hamlyn

Meat

Joanna Farrow

Notes

Both metric and imperial measurements have been given in all recipes.
Use one set of measurements only, and not a mixture of both.

Standard level spoon measurements are used in all recipes.
1 tablespoon = one 15 ml spoon
1 teaspoon = one 5 ml spoon

The Department of Health advises that eggs should not be consumed raw.
This book contains dishes made with raw or lightly cooked eggs. It is
prudent for vulnerable people such as pregnant and nursing mothers,
invalids, the elderly, babies and young children to avoid uncooked or lightly
cooked dishes made with eggs. Once prepared, these dishes should be kept
refrigerated and used promptly.

This book includes dishes made with nuts and nut derivatives. It is advisable
for customers with known allergic reactions to nuts and nut derivatives and
those who may be potentially vulnerable to these allergies, such as pregnant
and nursing mothers, invalids, the elderly, babies and children, to avoid
dishes made with nuts and nut oils. It is also prudent to check the labels of
pre-prepared ingredients for the possible inclusion of nut derivatives.

Ovens should be preheated to the specified temperature – if using a fan-
assisted oven, follow the manufacturer's instructions for adjusting the time
and the temperature.

First published in Great Britain in 2006 by Hamlyn,
a division of Octopus Publishing Group Ltd
2–4 Heron Quays, London E14 4JP

ISBN-13: 978-0-600-61262-9
ISBN-10: 0-600-61262-7

A CIP catalogue record for this book is available
from the British Library.

Printed and bound in China

10 9 8 7 6 5 4 3 2 1

Contents

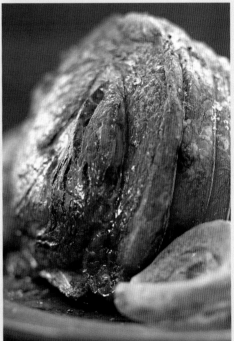

Introduction

Tenderness and flavour are the essence of good meat, and these qualities are largely determined by the animal's diet and the way it's slaughtered and hung. Consumers are becoming increasingly discerning about whether meat is wild or farmed, reared according to organic or battery principles, or raised indoors or outdoors. They are also beginning to want to know about the provenance and supplier of the meat they buy. Anyone who's cooked or eaten decent, flavour-packed meat will vouch for the difference between this and the cheaper, mass-produced cuts of meat. These are often from artificially reared stock, from an unknown source and usually prepacked for supermarkets, and they are not only very bland and flavourless, but also virtually impossible to cook with.

The most practical answer to sourcing good meat is to find a good butcher who cares about the quality of the meat and where it comes from, who will order special meats and prepare them for you, and who can advise you on the different cuts and the most suitable cooking methods. As with any food produce, the rewards of cooking and eating good-quality meat cannot be overemphasized.

Choosing

Bright red flesh is not necessarily a sign of quality. A deep, dark red flesh usually shows that the meat has been hung properly (see page 10). Look for a smooth outer layer of fat that is not too thick (after

all, you're paying for it) and a light marbling of fat through the lean flesh, which helps to baste the meat naturally during its cooking time. Choose neat, well-trimmed meat with no sign of jagged bones. Steaks and chops should be of an even thickness so they cook through at the same time. Never buy prepacked meat that has a grey tinge.

Storing

Most meats, especially larger pieces, will keep well in the refrigerator for several days. The exceptions are poultry, minced meat and offal, which should be cooked as soon as possible after buying. Never leave meat in the supermarket packaging it came in because it cannot breathe and will spoil more quickly. All meat should be loosened from its wrapping, particularly if it is in plastic, then transferred to a plate and lightly covered so that air can circulate. Store meat in the coldest part of the refrigerator.

Most meats freeze well, which is always worth remembering if you have an opportunity to buy a large quantity of organic meat directly from a farm or a market.

Cooking methods and techniques

The more expensive cuts of meat, taken from the least exercised parts of the body (usually the hindquarters), can be cooked fast, hot and dry – by roasting, grilling, frying and barbecuing, for example. The tougher cuts, usually from the most exercised parts of the body (the forequarters), are best cooked gently and slowly, partially or fully immersed in liquid. Some prime cuts can be cooked slowly in liquid, but cheaper cuts will never become tender if they are cooked quickly.

Roasting

Roast choice tender cuts on or off the bone, with or without stuffing. Sear a joint for roasting in oil first (in hot fat in the roasting tin on the hob or in a very hot oven) before you reduce the temperature to a moderate heat that will penetrate to the centre without burning the outside. Roasting times vary, depending on the type of meat, size and cut. If time allows, cook the meat from room temperature so that it heats through quickly.

Frying

Individual portions of tender meat – steak, escalopes and chops, for example – can be fried quickly so they're appetizingly browned on the outside and, for most people's tastes, still pink in the middle. Use a good-quality, sturdy pan and don't cram in too many pieces at once or the meat will steam in its own moisture. Season the meat on both sides first and get the oil or butter sizzling hot before you add the meat. Once cooked, the flavoursome residue and juices in the pan can be deglazed by adding wine or stock (see page 7).

Stir-frying

Meat for stir-frying should be cut into thin strips or slices and lightly seasoned. A wok is ideal so that you can give the meat a good stir without it falling out of the pan. Make sure that the fat is really hot before you add the meat and fry in small quantities if you're cooking a lot. Always stir-fry the meat before you add vegetables to the pan.

Pot-roasting and braising

Joints of meat that tend to be tough can be pot-roasted or braised on or off the bone, with or without stuffing. This is an excellent cooking method that allows flavours to mingle and because the cooking juices are so delicious, means you don't have to make a sauce or gravy. First, sear the joint on all sides in butter or oil, then cook it, covered, with a little stock, wine or beer and vegetables, herbs or spices, before cooking in the oven or on the hob. This method can also be used for choice cuts, such as rolled loin of pork, which leaves you free to get on with other things, confident that the gentle cooking process won't dry out or overcook the meat.

Stewing and casseroling

These cooking methods are similar; there's virtually no difference between them. Generally, stews are cooked on a hob and casseroles in an oven, although stews can be cooked in an oven, and can be left unattended. It's the best way to transform cheaper cuts of meat into fabulously tender dishes, and some stews will really benefit from cooking one day and then reheating the next. The key to success is thoroughly frying off the meat before you start stewing it.

Grilling

For straightforward, clean and easy cooking, grilling under an overhead grill is perfect, using the meat's integral fat to prevent it from drying out and doing away with the need for additional fat. Lightly season the meat before cooking and preheat the grill. Chargrilling is usually done on a gas- or electric-powered grill that imitates barbecuing. A ridged grill pan, preheated over the hob, is another very effective way of grilling (pictured below).

Flouring meat (pictured above)
Meat is sometimes floured before frying, which gives a good colour and thickens the cooking liquid. Make sure the meat is really dry first – pat it dry on kitchen paper if necessary – season the flour with a little salt and pepper and toss the meat in it until it is lightly dusted.

Poaching
Some meats, such as a joint of bacon, a brisket of beef or breast fillets of chicken can be cooked gently in water with additional vegetables and herbs so that they retain maximum moisture. The liquid can then be used in a sauce. It's vital that once the liquid has reached simmering point it's turned down to its lowest setting so that the meat is cooked as gently as possible. Meat that has been boiled for a long time will remain tough and chewy.

Frying off (pictured above right)
It's worth taking time to fry off pieces of meat if you're making a casserole or stew because it produces a good flavour and rich colour. Make sure the meat is thoroughly dry first and, if necessary, is floured and/or seasoned with salt and pepper. Heat the fat in a sturdy, heavy-based frying pan and add a batch of the meat. Don't try to fry off too much at once. The chunks of meat need plenty of space around them or they'll steam in their own juice. Use a wooden spatula to turn the meat once or twice during frying until it is deeply browned. Drain and transfer the meat with a slotted spoon while you fry the remainder.

Searing joints
Larger pieces of meat are usually seared before roasting or pot-roasting to add colour and keep in all the flavour. Pat the meat dry with kitchen paper if it's at all moist and season with salt and pepper. Heat the fat in a sturdy, heavy-based frying pan or roasting tin and sear the meat thoroughly on all sides until browned.

Deglazing
After frying or roasting meat there's plenty of flavour left in the pan or tin to form the base of a good sauce or gravy. Pour a little wine or stock (see pages 22–3) into the pan and cook over the hob, stirring with a wooden spatula as you scrape up the pan residue. If you're making gravy, the mixture can bubble for a few minutes so the liquid reduces and the flavour intensifies.

Basting

Traditionally, many meats, particularly roast joints, are basted (flooded with the pan juices) several times during cooking. This has the most beneficial effects on chicken, which develops a crisper, tastier skin as a result.

Using a meat thermometer

A meat thermometer enables you to detect whether a roasted joint has reached the right temperature and therefore has had the right amount of cooking. Insert the point of the thermometer into the thickest part of the joint, away from the bone (which would affect the reading), and leave it for 20–30 seconds. For pork, which must be served cooked through, it should read 70–75°C (158–167°F). For lamb and beef, it can range from 45°C (113°F) for very rare, through to 75°C (167°F) for well done.

Marinating

Marinades have only a minimal effect as meat tenderizers. Even acid ingredients, like lemon or orange juice and vinegar, cannot get through to the centre of the meat, and wine can sometimes even draw out moisture, resulting in a tougher texture. Marinades, wet or dry, are much better as flavour enhancers, penetrating meat with delicious aromatic ingredients, such as garlic, herbs and spices. They also give you an opportunity to prepare a dish in advance, perhaps first thing in the day, so it's ready for cooking, effortlessly, in the evening.

Resting meat

Resting a joint of meat after cooking is essential. This enables the muscle fibres to 'relax' after cooking, making the meat more tender and easier to carve. Transfer the meat to a serving platter, cover with

Roasting chart for meats

Unless the recipe states otherwise, roast the joint at 220°C (425°F), Gas Mark 7 for 15 minutes, then reduce the cooking time to 180°C (350°F), Gas Mark 4 and cook for the following times. The heat indications show the internal meat temperature.

Beef	(rare)	10 minutes per 500 g (1 lb)	45°C (112°F)
	(medium)	15 minutes per 500 g (1 lb)	60°C (140°F)
	(well done)	20 minutes per 500 g (1 lb)	75°C (165°F)
Veal		15 minutes per 500 g (1 lb)	70°C (158°F)
Lamb	(rare)	10 minutes per 500 g (1 lb)	45°C (113°F)
	(medium)	15 minutes per 500 g (1 lb)	60°C (140°F)
	(well done)	20 minutes per 500 g (1 lb)	75°C (165°F)
Pork		25–30 minutes per 500 g (1 lb)	75°C (165°F)

foil and leave for 20–30 minutes, depending on the size of the joint. This gives you plenty of time to make the gravy and finish cooking any vegetables.

Carving

There are recognized ways of carving the different cuts of meat, but the golden rule is to use a decent, sharp carving knife, preferably paired with a pronged fork to hold the meat in place. Making sure the meat has rested first (see above) is essential, as is cutting across the grain of the meat to produce the most tender slices. Work on a firm, flat surface so that the meat doesn't slip about (a board with a gully round the edges is ideal) and remove any string or skewers first.

Homemade mince

For burgers and other dishes that use minced beef, lamb, pork or veal, home mincing will ensure a good texture with just enough fat to keep the meat moist. You'll also know exactly what's gone into the mince. The choice of cut used depends largely on the dish – for example, you might want good-quality steak mince for burgers but a cheaper cut for meat sauce. (See the appropriate beef, veal, lamb and pork chapters.) Prepare the meat by cutting it into small chunks, discarding any large pieces of fat, but not all of it. Chop in the food processor in small batches or use an old-fashioned meat mincer. A good butcher will mince your choice of meat cut for you.

Beef

For the best flavour and texture beef should be hung after slaughter for at least two weeks. During this time the enzymes and bacteria in the meat break down the fibres, making the meat more tender, deepening the colour of the flesh and giving it time to develop flavour. It also loses moisture so that it's easier to cook with and produces less shrinkage and spluttering. To keep down costs, much of the beef produced today is not hung properly, which makes it tasteless and watery. Choose beef that's marbled with streaks of fat, which helps it to stay succulent.

Best cuts for roasting

Fore rib Resembling a huge chop, this is a prime cut for roasting on the bone as it's lean and tender but is marbled with fat and absorbs plenty of flavour from the bone. Also available boned and rolled. Ask your butcher to chine the backbone for you (this means sawing through the bones to detach the backbone from the ribs) so that carving is easier.

Wing rib Taken from behind the fore rib, this cut can be roasted or cut into Porterhouse steaks.

Sirloin Either sold on the bone or boned and rolled, this is leaner than rib, but is still very tender.

Fillet (tenderloin) A very tender, expensive cut, but it does not have as much flavour as other prime cuts because of its leanness. It is best cooked rare as it tends to dry out during cooking.

Best cuts for pot-roasting and braising

Top rump (thick flank) This can be pot-roasted in a piece or thinly sliced for frying or stir-frying.

Topside (round steak) (pictured left) A lean cut taken from the thigh, with little fat. A really choice piece of topside, barded by the butcher (that is, wrapped in thin sheets of fat to keep it moist), can be used successfully as a roasting joint, but it does have a tendency to dryness.

Silverside A less tender cut than topside, taken from the back of the thigh, this is delicious for pot-roasting. Silverside can also be bought salted and spiced.

Brisket Taken from the breast and usually sold boned and rolled, it is often salted. Order this well in advance from the butcher or salt your own (see page 42).

Best cuts for frying and grilling

Fillet steak A very lean and tender cut from the fillet. The steaks are called *filets* *mignons* if cut from the thin end or *tournedos* if taken from further up the fillet. Chateaubriand, cut from the thickest end of a large fillet, is a hefty steak that usually serves two.

Sirloin steak A large, well-flavoured steak with a layer of fat running along one edge. Entrecôte steak is cut from the middle of the sirloin.

Rump steak (pictured above) A large, well-flavoured steak with a layer of fat running along one edge. It has a much firmer texture than sirloin.

T-bone steak This combines the end of the sirloin with fillet and a small T-shaped bone.

Porterhouse steak Cut from the wing rib end of the sirloin.

Rib-eye steak Cut from the eye of the fore rib, this has more fat than other steaks but excellent flavour.

Best cuts for slow cooking

Chuck (blade) A juicy, well-flavoured, lean cut, taken from the shoulder region. Usually sold sliced or cubed for braising, stewing and pies.

Short ribs Taken from the forequarter flank, this cut has plenty of flavour and is best slowly braised so that the meat falls off the bone.

Neck and clod A cheap, sinewy cut used for stewing and good for the stock pot.

Flank Underside behind the breast, it is often trimmed of fat and made into mince.

Skirt (flank steak) A leaner part of flank with plenty of flavour but needing

very slow cooking. A good choice for pies and puddings.

Shin (foreleg) Gelatinous stewing meat with good flavour, this requires long, gentle cooking.

Leg (hock, hough) Similar to shin, this requires the same long, gentle cooking.

Minced beef This can be taken from any cuts but usually comes from the cheaper ones, like neck and flank. Leaner steak mince can be taken from any of the superior cuts, such as chuck. Look for mince with a good, rich colour, which denotes less fat, or buy the cut of your choice and make your own (see page 9).

Oxtail Sold cut into chunky lengths for making into wintry stews and soups, oxtail needs long, gentle cooking so it's tender and falling from the bone. Best made a day in advance so that the layer of fat that sets on the surface can be easily removed.

Ox kidney Dark and strongly flavoured, ox kidney is used in small quantities in steak and kidney pie.

Ox liver A coarse, strongly flavoured liver, which needs very slow, gentle cooking to make it palatable more tender. Can be minced for pâtés.

Perfect steaks

Before you cook the meat, heat the fat (butter with a dash of oil is ideal) until it's sizzling in a heavy-based frying pan or ridged grill pan. Add the thoroughly dry, seasoned steak and leave it to cook completely on one side before turning it. Avoid the urge to keep flipping the steak over. Don't overfill the pan with meat or the temperature will lower and the meat will steam in its own juice.

Cooking times for steaks 2 cm (¾ inch) thick

Blue Cook very briefly on each side until seared but completely rare in the centre.
Rare 1½ minutes on each side until heated through but very pink in the centre.
Medium rare 2½ minutes on each side or until most of the steak is cooked with just a thin band of pink running through the centre.
Medium to well done 5 minutes on each side until completely cooked through but still moist.

Roasting beef

Bring a roasting joint to room temperature before cooking. Because many beef roasts are cooked quickly, the temperature it starts off at will affect the 'doneness' of the finished roast. Roast beef at a high temperature, about 220°C (425°F), Gas Mark 7, for 15 minutes, then reduce the temperature to 180°C (350°F), Gas Mark 4, and cook for 12–13 minutes per 500 g (1 lb) for rare, 17–18 minutes per 500 g (1 lb) for medium and 22–24 minutes per 500 g (1 lb) for well done.

Veal

This meat comes from milk-fed calves, which are slaughtered when they are between eight and twelve weeks old, or from slightly older (four to five months old), grass-fed calves. All veal should be pale and moist-looking without any sign of redness. The meat should be very lean with a little marbling of fat that's similar in colour to the flesh.

Best cuts for roasting

Leg Taken from the hind legs, this cut is sold in smaller joints as for beef. It is best roasted under a layer of fat bacon, or barded to counteract any dryness, or pot-roasted with vegetables.

Loin This expensive roasting joint can be cooked on the bone or boned and rolled, with or without stuffing. It may contain the tenderloin (see below) and kidneys.

Best cuts for frying and grilling

Escalopes These thin steaks are usually cut from the fillet end of the leg, although they can also be taken from any other lean cut. Escalopes are often pounded before cooking to flatten and tenderize them (pictured right).

Tenderloin Often removed from the loin for selling separately, the tenderloin can be cut into chunky slices, or else into medallions.

Loin chops Large chops, cut from the loin, are good for frying, grilling or barbecuing.

Best cuts for pot-roasting, braising and stewing

Middle neck Usually sold as cutlets.

Chump Taken from the area between the top of the leg and the loin, chump is usually sold boned and rolled for slow cooking.

Shoulder Usually sold boned and rolled for pot-roasting.

Breast Traditionally boned and rolled for long, slow pot-roasting.

Shin Foreleg of veal, most famously used in *Osso bucco* (see page 51); the central bone contains deliciously soft marrow.

Minced veal Usually cut from the neck or scrag end.

Liver Calf's liver, the most prized of all the livers, has a delicate flavour and unblemished texture. It is best fried briefly in butter.

Preparing escalopes

Veal escalopes are used widely in Italian cooking and can be prepared from leg steaks. To prepare, place each slice between two sheets of clingfilm and beat until flattened with a rolling pin or meat mallet to tenderize the meat as thoroughly as possible.

Lamb

The texture and flavour of lamb for cooking depends very much on the age of the animal at slaughter. Young lamb, under the age of one year, is generally considered to be the best, although older meat has as much, if not more, flavour. These older meats, which require more gentle cooking, are known as hoggit (over one year old) or mutton (two to three years old).

Best cuts for roasting

Leg This varies in size from a small, whole leg of about 1 kg (2 lb) to a larger one of up to 2.5–2.7 kg (5–6 lb), which might be sold halved as fillet (thick end) or shank (thin end). It can also be sold completely boned or part-boned for presentation (when the shank bone is left intact), which takes the hassle out of carving around the central bone. A boned leg can also be opened out – butterflied – so it can be cooked faster or even barbecued whole. Let your butcher know a day or two in advance if you want the leg boned or butterflied.

Chump Taken from between the leg and the loin, this cut can sometimes be bought as a separate cut for roasting.

Shoulder Fattier than the other prime cuts, shoulder makes a sweet, juicy roast that benefits from a longer roasting. Occasionally it can be bought boned and stuffed, making a melon-shaped roast called a ballotine.

Rack of lamb (best end) (pictured left) Taken from the loin end of the ribs, this is a joint of seven or eight ribs. Ask your butcher to chine it for you (saw through the bones to detach the backbone from the ribs) so that carving is easier. A rack of lamb, or the cutlets taken from the rack, can be French-trimmed for presentation – that is, the thin end of each rib is scraped clean (see opposite). Two racks fitted together with rib ends linked make up a guard of honour, while two racks formed into a round (with or without stuffing packed in the centre) make up a crown of lamb. A rack of lamb can also be boned and rolled for roasting.

Loin On the bone or boned and rolled, loin of lamb is one of the most expensive cuts. Two joined loins on the bone make up a saddle of lamb, an impressive roasting joint for a special meal.

Best cuts for grilling, frying and barbecuing

Chops Taken from the loin, these meaty

chops have a small, T-shaped bone in the centre.

Cutlets Taken from the rack of lamb, these are far less meaty than loin chops, and you should allow at least three per person.

Noisettes A boned and rolled rack of lamb, secured with string then cut into chunky slices.

Leg steaks With their central bone, these lean steaks are particularly good for barbecuing.

Chump chops Juicy chops with bone in the centre.

Neck fillet (tenderloin) A well-flavoured, long, slender cut from the neck, this can be sliced and pan-fried once any fat has been removed or used in stews and hot pots.

Liver Tender and delicious, lamb's liver is second to calf's liver and is best fried in butter after cutting out any membrane and tubes.

Kidneys Mild, tender and delicious fried in butter.

Best cuts for stewing and braising

Scrag This inexpensive cut has more bone, gristle and fat than other cuts but plenty of flavour, so it is a good choice for soups and stews. If it's really fatty, it's best made in advance and cooled so that the layer of fat can be removed before reheating.

Breast A thin, cheap cut of lamb, consisting of layers of lean and fat with plenty of flavour. A meatier piece of breast can be successfully rolled and roasted.

Middle neck A fattier cut taken from near the shoulder blade and next to the best end. It is used for stews and hotpots.

Minced lamb Taken from the shoulder, middle neck and other cheaper cuts for making *Shepherd's pie* (see page 72), *Moussaka* (see page 73) and burgers. Buy ready-made mince or make your own.

French trimming a rack of lamb

If it has not already been done by your butcher, a whole loin or rack of lamb can be trimmed for presentation. Cut off 5 cm (2 inches) of the flesh from the ends of the ribs. Cut away the meat from between the ribs, then scrape off any meat that clings to the bones.

Removing fat from stews

Once cooked, turn the stew or casserole into a container to cool. Chill until the fat forms a solid layer on top. Lift off the fat and return the stew to the dish to reheat.

Cutting away excess fat

Use a sharp knife to trim off most of the fat from cuts such as chops, neck fillet, breast or shoulder before cooking. Leave a thin layer of fat around the meat to add flavour and succulence.

Pork
This is the cheapest of the mainstream meats and, with chicken, has suffered most from intensive farming, often resulting in plump meat that is not hung and has little flavour. Most pigs are slaughtered when they're several months old (known as porkers), except for suckling pig, popular in Spain, where the pigs are slaughtered at three to eight weeks.

Best cuts for roasting and pot-roasting

Leg A whole leg of pork is generally too large to roast so is divided into fillet (butt) end and shank (knuckle) end. On larger animals these joints are often cut into smaller, boneless pieces for smaller roasts. The leg contains less fat than other cuts of pork, so take extra care when cooking to prevent it from drying out.

Loin This tender, delicate cut is delicious on or off the bone. It can be boned and rolled, with or without stuffing. Like the leg, this cut is also relatively lean.

Chump end This cut can be roasted on or off the bone.

Shoulder (blade) A multi-purpose cut, this can be roasted, pot-roasted or cut into steaks for grilling, frying or barbecuing.

Best cuts for frying, grilling and barbecuing

Loin chops Taken from the loin, those from the hind end often have a slice of the kidney attached.

Chump chops Chunky, juicy chops taken from the chump end.

Tenderloin (fillet) On larger pigs the fillet can be removed and sold as a separate cut. Tender and meaty, it can be sliced into medallions for grilling or frying. A very large fillet, weighing about 500 g (1 lb), can be wrapped in bacon and roasted.

Best cuts for slow cooking

Hand and spring An awkwardly shaped, cheaper cut from the front legs, this can be sold in one piece, but more frequently is cut up for stewing and mince.

Spare ribs Taken from the upper part of the ribcage, this is sold in sheets or cut into individual ribs. Chinese spare ribs, which are taken from the lower ribcage, cook to a delicious, melting succulence when bathed in a sweet tangy glaze. Allow plenty per portion because of the bones.

Belly Fatty but full flavoured and often sold salted, this can be casseroled in chunks or minced for pâtés. A lean piece can also be roasted or grilled.

Diced or pie pork This can be taken from any cut, often from the fillet end of the leg or the shoulder, and is good for curries, pies, casseroles and kebabs.

Minced pork This is made from cheaper cuts, such as shoulder or hand and spring.

Liver Strongly flavoured and coarse in texture, pigs' liver can be soaked in milk before use to tone down the flavour. It's usually kept for mincing into pâtés.

Kidneys Strongly flavoured but tender enough to slow cook in casseroles.

Ham (pictured above right)
Most ham comes from the hind legs. In its raw, cured state, this is known as gammon;

when it's cooked, ham. Other cooked, cured cuts, such as shoulder cuts, are also called ham. The leg cuts contain less fat, while the shoulder is marbled with fat, but has a good flavour. Ready-cooked hams can be bought whole or sliced. Those bought for home cooking should be soaked for at least 24 hours (or up to several days if they're large) before cooking to remove excess saltiness. They're then cooked in water or stock with vegetables for eating hot or cold, or finished in the oven with a sweet, tangy glaze to add flavour and enhance appearance.

Pork can also be cured for eating uncooked and very thinly sliced. Italian prosciutto is the most familiar of these, of which Parma ham is considered the best. These are cured and then air-dried for several months.

Bacon

Available both smoked or unsmoked (green) this can be bought in the piece or sliced. Because most of the flavour comes from the fat, belly pork is widely used for bacons, such as Italian pancetta, German and Scandinavian Speck, Spanish Tocino or streaky bacon. Leaner cuts come from meatier parts of the pig, such as the back. All bacon is cooked before eating.

Salted meat

Salted meats, usually pork and beef, can be ordered from the butcher, or home cured (see page 42). Traditionally used as a preserving technique, salted meats are now widely used for their distinctive flavour.

Crackling

Crackling can be achieved only on good-quality pork with firm, dry skin. Store the joint in the refrigerator, loosely wrapped so the skin remains dry. This is particularly important if you've bought a tightly wrapped piece of meat. If the skin has not already been scored, use a very sharp knife to score the skin at 1 cm (½ inch) intervals. (Do this in the same direction as the meat will be carved.) Rub the skin with plenty of sea salt before roasting.

Stuffing and rolling

A boned roasting or pot-roasting joint can be stuffed and rolled before cooking, even if you've bought the meat ready rolled from the butcher. Untie the meat and spread it with the cooled stuffing. Roll up the meat around the stuffing and secure it at 3 cm (1¼ inch) intervals with string.

Poultry
All poultry, which includes chicken, turkey, goose, duck and guinea fowl, has been subjected to intensive farming to satisfy the demands from the supermarkets to supply inexpensive meat. As with all meat, the difference in flavour and goodness – as well as in the animals' welfare – of mass-produced poultry and 'real' poultry is staggering.

Chicken

Chicken is one of the most versatile meats. The lean texture and relatively mild flavour makes it incredibly 'useful' to cook, from a simple roast to hot, spicy, aromatic dishes. A specific farm or breed label is a good guide to quality. Although more expensive, you can still be quite thrifty with a decent chicken. Buy a large one and you can serve it roasted one day and tossed with a salad the next. The bones, trimmings and giblets can be made into a delicious stock base for soup (see page 23), with any leftover meat and plenty of vegetables added to make a third meal.

Poussins and yellow-fleshed, corn-fed chickens are also subject to intensive farming, so look for free-range or organic labels on the packs when buying.

Turkey

Although traditionally served at festive occasions, turkey is always a lean and economical choice. Usually sold whole, the breast meat can be sold as a piece, in steaks or in strips for stir-frying. It makes a suitable substitute for chicken in most spicy dishes. Allow 350 g (11½ oz) weight per serving, for a whole roasted turkey.

Goose

There's very little meat per kilo/pound on an oven-ready goose, because much of it is fat that's cooked off during roasting. A 5–6 kg (10–12 lb) goose will serve up to 10 people. Rich in flavour, goose is usually partnered with tangy, light stuffings and accompaniments such as apples, raisins and chestnuts. Before roasting, prick the skin to let the fat melt out, and pull out the lumps of fat in the cavity. Roast the goose and the removed fat on a rack over the roasting tin. When cooking a goose, there is a huge amount of valuable fat that collects and can be stored in the fridge for dripping. Use it on bread, for roasting potatoes or for cassoulets and confits.

Duck

Duck is richly flavoured but contains a high percentage of fat, with most of the meat on the breast fillets. A duck weighing about 2.5 kg (5 lb) will serve four people. Always prick the skin with a skewer before roasting to let the fat melt out and roast it on a rack over the roasting tin. Some duck are specially reared for Chinese-style duck recipes and are labelled accordingly – Peking Duck, for example.

Guinea fowl

Guinea fowl, which tastes like slightly gamey chicken, can be used instead of chicken when you're looking for something more unusual. As with chicken, the flavour varies greatly between intensively farmed and free-range birds.

Poultry livers

Poultry livers should come with the giblets when you buy a whole bird. Use them in stock, fry in butter or add to pâtés or stuffings. Chicken livers are widely available and can be bought fresh or frozen. Use liver from free-range birds if possible.

Trussing (pictured above)

Trussing poultry helps to maintain a good shape during roasting and stops the leg meat from drying out. Remove any plastic trussing and fill the cavity with stuffing, if using in the recipe. Stretch the neck flap under the bird and fold back the wing tips to hold the flap in place.

Position the bird with the neck cavity facing you and pull a long piece of string under the bird, bringing the ends up on either side between the legs and wings. Take the string back between the legs and breasts and hook it under the ends of each drumstick, bringing them around the outside of the drumsticks. Firmly tie the ends together over the cavity. Loop the ends under the parson's nose and tie together once more.

Jointing chicken and guinea fowl (pictured above right)

Cut off the legs through the joints, bending the legs back as you work so the leg sockets are more visible. Place the legs, skin side down, on the board and cut the drumstick from the thigh. (This is easier if you bend the legs back and forth so that you can see more clearly where the joint is.) Make a cut down one side of the breastbone, then ease the breast meat away from the bone, keeping the knife as close to the bone as possible to avoid wastage. Cut through the joint where the wing is attached. Repeat on the other side. Cut the wings from the breast meat, taking a little of the breast meat with it. If liked, halve each breast widthways.

Skewering a duck or goose

Place the bird, breast side down, on a board and prick it all over with a fine skewer so the fat can run out during roasting. For presentation, avoid pricking the breast area.

Checking the bird is cooked

Chicken, turkey and guinea fowl must always be thoroughly cooked through. To ensure they are cooked properly, push a skewer through the thickest part of the thigh. If the juices run clear, the bird is cooked. If they are still pink, return to the oven for a little longer.

Spatchcocking

Small chickens, poussins and game birds can be spatchcocked, which involves splitting and flattening them out to make it easier to grill or barbecue them. Use kitchen scissors or shears to cut off the wing tips, then cut through the bony meat on either side of the backbone. Discard the backbone and flatten out the bird by pushing down on the breastbone with the heel of your hand. On larger birds you can retain their flattened shape by pushing a couple of long skewers horizontally through the meat.

Game and other meats

Game, furred or feathered, is becoming more popular as an interesting and healthy alternative to other meats. Most game is protected by law (which varies from region to region) to prevent the animals from being over-hunted or shot and to allow for the rearing of their young.

Venison

Venison is the meat taken from roe, fallow or red deer and is available both wild and farmed. The hanging time determines the 'gaminess' of the flavour, and this can range from several days to up to three weeks. Saddle, loin and leg (haunch) of venison are the choice cuts for roasting, while the other more sinewy parts are often sold diced for pâtés, pies and casseroles. Venison sausages are also widely available.

Buy meat that's dark and close grained. Venison has a tendency to dryness and can benefit from barding or marinating.

Rabbit (pictured below)

The strength of flavour of rabbit can depend both on the animal's age and whether it is wild or farmed. Rabbit is best not eaten when too young, because the flavour will not have had time to develop, but it can be eaten without hanging first. Widely used in Spanish cooking, rabbit

can be roasted with olive oil and herbs or cooked with wine and garlic. Rabbit pie is still a traditional English country speciality, flavoured with robust ingredients like bacon and mustard. An average-sized rabbit will comfortably serve two people.

Hare

Leverets (hares under one year old) are the most tender and delicious, after which they start to toughen, so might need longer cooking. Hare is a much darker meat than rabbit and should be hung for several days before use. Because of its dry texture, it is best either marinated or wrapped in fat (or both) before slow roasting or casseroling. Dress up with flavours like red wine, port, juniper, cloves and redcurrant jelly.

Wild boar

Wild boar is best eaten young, tasting a little like a gamey pork, and, like pork, is equally suited to fruity accompaniments. The flesh should be very dark with little fat. If young, hanging is sufficient to tenderize, but older meat needs marinating as well. Legs and saddle can be roasted; other cuts grilled, fried or braised. Boar must be cooked through before eating.

Pigeon

Pigeon has a richly flavoured, deep red flesh that toughens up on older birds and can be tenderized by marinating in red wine. Only the breasts have any meat worth bothering with. These can easily be removed; use the rest of the carcass for well-flavoured stock. Allow one to two birds per serving.

Quail (pictured above)

Small and mildly flavoured, quail is fiddly to prepare and usually served whole, sometimes stuffed, or with sauces using ingredients like raisins, sherry and crème fraîche. In some Mediterranean countries they're served wrapped in vine leaves. Allow two per portion unless really large.

Partridge

This has a more delicate flavour than most birds, so is best accompanied with similarly delicate flavourings. Like pigeon, most of the meat is on the breasts, which can be removed and the rest consigned to a well-flavoured stock. Allow one bird per serving.

Grouse

Grouse is one of the most prized and expensive of the game birds, and it has a relatively short season. Younger grouse taste best when they are simply roasted with a covering of bacon to keep them moist; older birds often benefit from marinating or are added to game pies and casseroles. Allow one per serving.

Pheasant

Pheasant are often bought as a brace, which consists of the slightly larger male and smaller, juicer female. A pheasant that has not been hung will taste marginally more gamey than a chicken, while one that's been hung for several weeks will have an extremely strong flavour. Young pheasant can be wrapped in bacon and roasted, while older birds are best pot-roasted or used in pies and casseroles. Most average-sized pheasants will serve two, but a larger cock can sometimes serve three.

Goat

Goat has a flavour that can be likened to lamb, for which it can be a good substitute in spicy lamb casseroles and stews. It can be difficult to get hold of it in your local supermarket and you may need to order it from a specialist supplier.

Ostrich

Ostrich has become popular as a lean, tender alternative to mainstream meats, although it's generally harder to find. Prime ostrich steaks can be pan-fried, just as you'd cook beef, while tougher cuts are best added to stews and casseroles.

Preparing game birds for roasting

To prepare a young game bird for a simple roast, remove any stray feathers and season the bird inside and out. Tuck herbs such as rosemary, sage, tarragon, parsley or thyme into the cavity and lay strips of fat bacon over the breast. Roast in a hot oven, 200°C (400°F), Gas Mark 6, for between 15 and 45 minutes, depending on the size of the bird. Test by piercing the flesh between the thigh and breast to see if the meat is cooked.

Removing breast meat

For small birds, such as partridge or pigeon, use a sharp knife to cut down one side of the breastbone and carefully ease the meat away.

Basic recipes *So many meat dishes rely on a well-flavoured stock that it makes sense to make your own when bones and trimmings are available. If you're short of time or you want to collect plenty of bones to make a large stock pot, bag them up and freeze until needed. Stocks keep in the refrigerator for a few days and freeze well for several months.*

Beef stock *Unless you're roasting a large piece of beef on the bone, ask your butcher to saw up some marrow bones for you. Add cheap cuts of beef or trimmings to boost flavour. Brown raw bones in a hot oven first.*

PREPARATION TIME: 10 minutes

COOKING TIME: about 3 hours

MAKES: about 1 litre (1¾ pints)

750 g (1½ lb) beef bones

1 large onion, roughly chopped

2 large carrots, roughly sliced

2 celery sticks, roughly sliced

1 teaspoon black peppercorns

several bay leaves and thyme sprigs

1 Put the bones in a large, heavy-based saucepan with the onion, carrots, celery, peppercorns and herbs. Just cover with cold water and bring slowly to the boil.

2 Reduce the heat and simmer very gently for about 3 hours, skimming the surface if necessary.

3 Strain through a large sieve and leave to cool, then chill so that the fat can easily be removed from the surface.

Jellied stock *Pork makes a really good gelatinous stock because it's rich in collagen, which converts to gelatine on heating. It's worth making your own, which is far tastier than adding gelatine to a liquid stock.*

PREPARATION TIME: 10 minutes

COOKING TIME: 2–2½ hours

MAKES: about 750 ml (1¼ pints)

500 g (1 lb) raw pork bones, including at least 1 pig's trotter

1 onion, roughly chopped

2 carrots, roughly sliced

2 celery sticks, roughly sliced

1 glass of white wine

3 bay leaves

3 sprigs of sage

1 Put the bones and trotter in a roasting tin and roast in a preheated oven, 200°C (400°F), Gas Mark 6, for 15 minutes. Add the vegetables and roast for a further 5 minutes.

2 Tip the ingredients and juices into a large saucepan. Pour the wine into the roasting tin and stir to scrape up the sediment. Add to the saucepan with the herbs and just cover with water.

3 Bring just to the boil, reduce the heat and simmer gently for 2–2½ hours. Strain, then leave to cool then and chill.

Chicken stock
Never throw away a chicken carcass. Cooked or raw, it makes a fabulous stock. Use all bones, skin and pan scrapings from a roast. If using a raw carcass, brown for about 30 minutes in a hot oven.

PREPARATION TIME: 10 minutes

COOKING TIME: 1½–2 hours

MAKES: about 1 litre (1¾ pints)

1 large chicken carcass, including any trimmings (e.g., neck, heart and gizzard if available)

1 onion, roughly chopped

1 large carrot, roughly chopped

several bay leaves

1 teaspoon black peppercorns

1 Pack the chicken carcass into a large saucepan, crushing the bones if necessary to make it fit. Add the trimmings, vegetables, bay leaves and peppercorns. Just cover with cold water.

2 Bring slowly to the boil, then reduce the heat and simmer very gently for 1½–2 hours. Strain, then cool and chill or freeze.

Game stock
Use any mixture of game, feathered or furred. The leftovers from small birds, like pigeon and partridge (of which you've just used the breasts), make great additions to a game stock.

PREPARATION TIME: 10 minutes

COOKING TIME: 1½ hours

MAKES: about 750 ml (1¼ pints)

500 g (1 lb) game trimmings (e.g., carcasses, necks, wings)

1 large onion, roughly chopped

1 large carrot, roughly sliced

2 celery sticks or chunk of celeriac, roughly chopped

1 glass of red wine

1 teaspoon juniper berries, lightly crushed

2 bay leaves and several sprigs of thyme

1 If you're using raw game trimmings, put them in a roasting tin and cook in a preheated oven, 200°C (400°F), Gas Mark 6, for 15 minutes.

2 Tip the trimmings into a large saucepan and add the remaining ingredients. Just cover with cold water and bring to the boil. Reduce the heat and simmer very gently for 1½ hours.

3 Strain, cool and chill.

Variations

Duck or turkey stock Use the same method as for chicken stock. Although these have a more distinctive flavour (and so are not as versatile as chicken stock) they're useful for roast turkey or duck gravies, soups and casseroles.

Veal stock Use the same method as for beef stock, using raw bone if liked for a lighter, general purpose stock. Veal stock usually jellies naturally, even after freezing and reheating, so it can also be used for pâtés.

Lamb stock Use the same method as for beef stock, roasting raw bone first with any scraps of meat. It's not as versatile as chicken or beef stock and is generally only used in lamb dishes.

Gravy

Good-quality cuts of roasted meat or poultry provide delicious fats and juices for a well-flavoured gravy. After roasting, drain the meat, cover it with foil, and make the gravy while the meat stands.

COOKING TIME: 5 minutes

MAKES: about 600 ml (1 pint)

pan juices from roasted meat

1 tablespoon plain flour (less for a thin gravy)

300–400 ml (10–14 fl oz) liquid (this could be water, drained from the accompanying vegetables; stock; half stock and half water; or half wine and half water)

salt and pepper

1 Tilt the roasting tin and skim off the fat from the surface with a large serving spoon until you're left with the pan juices and just a thin layer of fat.

2 Sprinkle the flour into the tin and stir with a wooden spoon over a moderate heat, scraping up all the residue, particularly from around the edges.

3 Gradually pour the liquid into the tin, stirring well until the gravy is thick and glossy. Let the mixture bubble, then check the seasoning, adding a little salt and pepper if necessary.

Variations

For lamb or game gravy, a spoonful of redcurrant jelly adds a subtle sweetness. For pork try apple jelly and cider instead of stock. To sharpen up a rich, fatty gravy add a squeeze of lemon juice. A teaspoon of mustard makes a good addition to beef gravy.

Shortcrust pastry

Use this buttery pastry recipe for covering any meat pies. It keeps in the refrigerator for a day and should be used to cover a cooled pie filling. Use a lipped pie dish so the pastry doesn't slip.

PREPARATION TIME: 20 minutes
COOKING TIME: 45 minutes–1 hour
MAKES: 275 g (9 oz)

175 g (6 oz) plain flour
50 g (2 oz) butter, diced
50 g (2oz) lard, diced
1 teaspoon iced water
salt
milk, to glaze

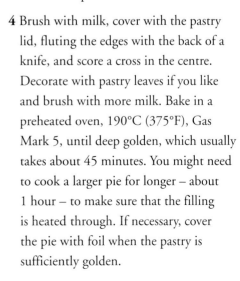

1 Put the flour and a pinch of salt in a mixing bowl. Add the fats and rub them in with your fingertips until the mixture looks like coarse breadcrumbs.

2 Use a round-bladed knife to stir in the iced water until the mixture starts to bind together. Use your hands to bring the mixture into a dough, adding a little more water if it feels dry. Lightly knead the dough on a floured surface until it is smooth. Wrap and chill until needed.

3 Roll out the pastry on a lightly floured surface until it is 5 cm (2 inches) larger than the pie dish. Cut a 2.5 cm (1 inch) strip from around the edges and place it on the dampened rim of the dish.

4 Brush with milk, cover with the pastry lid, fluting the edges with the back of a knife, and score a cross in the centre. Decorate with pastry leaves if you like and brush with more milk. Bake in a preheated oven, 190°C (375°F), Gas Mark 5, until deep golden, which usually takes about 45 minutes. You might need to cook a larger pie for longer – about 1 hour – to make sure that the filling is heated through. If necessary, cover the pie with foil when the pastry is sufficiently golden.

Beef and veal *Good-quality succulent beef needs little in the way of additional flavourings. Lightly seasoned and roasted or pan fried, the meat and cooking juices will be packed with flavour. Peppery ingredients like mustard and horseradish make classic companions, as do red wine, beer, anchovies, carrots, thyme and parsley.*

Veal has a more delicate flavour than beef, and because of its leanness, has a tendency towards dryness so often needs additional fat. Butchers sometimes 'bard' veal joints (wrap them in thin sheets of fat to keep them moist), or the meat can be cooked with additional fat like olive oil, butter or bacon. Veal can be enhanced by distinct flavours like citrus fruits, smoked ham, cheese or anchovies.

Roast beef and Yorkshire puddings

If cooking roast potatoes, use a separate tin and put it on the top shelf of the oven for the final hour's roasting. Move to the lower shelf while cooking the Yorkshires.

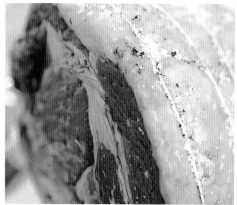

PREPARATION TIME: 20 minutes

COOKING TIME: 1¼–2½ hours

SERVES: 6–8

1.5–2 kg (3–4 lb) rib or sirloin of beef, on the bone or boned and rolled

dripping or lard

150 ml (¼ pint) beef stock

150 ml (¼ pint) red wine

salt and pepper

Yorkshire puddings

125 g (4 oz) plain flour

2 eggs

300 ml (½ pint) milk

1 Weigh the meat and calculate the cooking time (see page 8). Put it in a roasting tin with the fat uppermost and rub all over with a little seasoning. Roast in a preheated oven, 220°C (425°F), Gas Mark 7, for 15 minutes. Reduce the heat to 180°C (350°F), Gas Mark 4, and cook for the calculated time.

2 Meanwhile, make the pudding batter. Mix the flour with a little salt in a bowl and break the eggs into the centre. Add half the milk and gradually whisk in the flour and then the remaining milk to make a smooth batter. Leave to stand.

3 Transfer the beef to a serving platter, cover and leave to stand. Raise the heat to 220°C (425°F), Gas Mark 7. Dot a little lard or dripping (or fat from the roasting tin) into sections of a Yorkshire pudding tin and put in the oven until very hot. Pour in the batter and cook for 20–25 minutes until risen and golden.

4 Heat the stock and wine in the tin with the meat juices, scraping up the residue. Bring to the boil and pour into a jug.

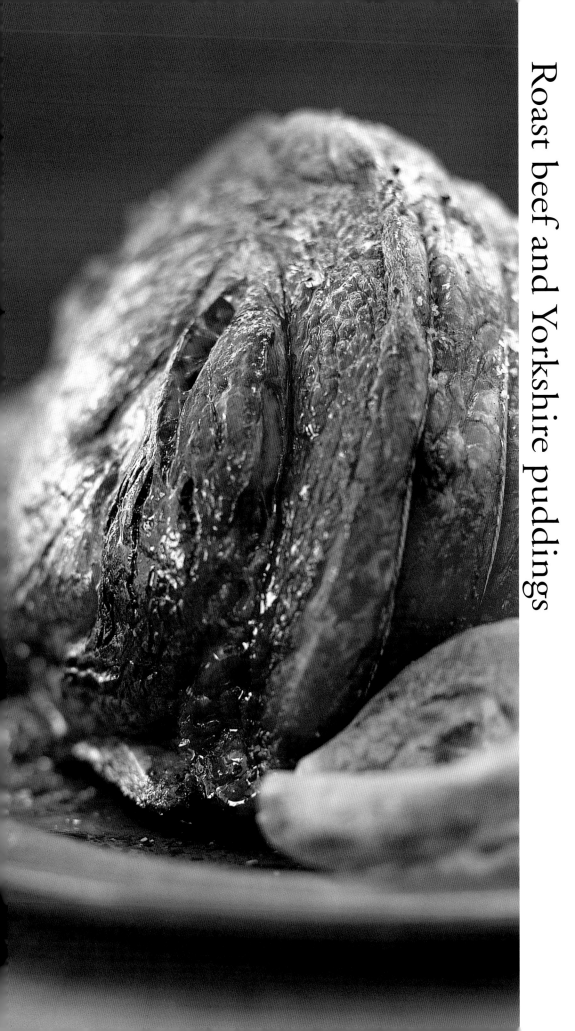

Roast beef and Yorkshire puddings

Steak and mushroom pie

Cook the filling a day in advance so it's cool for the pastry topping. Substitute 200 g (7 oz) diced beef kidney for some of the meat for traditional steak and kidney pie.

PREPARATION TIME: 40 minutes, plus cooling

COOKING TIME: 2½ hours

SERVES: 4

3 tablespoons plain flour

750 g (1½ lb) stewing steak, diced

50 g (2 oz) butter

1 large onion, chopped

2 garlic cloves, crushed

450 ml (¾ pint) stout

150 ml (¼ pint) beef stock

2 bay leaves

1 tablespoon hot horseradish sauce

250 g (8 oz) cup mushrooms

single quantity shortcrust pastry (see page 25)

milk, to glaze

salt and pepper

1 Season the flour and use it to coat the steak. Heat a dot of the butter in a large, heavy-based frying pan and fry the meat in batches until it is well browned, using a slotted spoon to drain and transfer each batch to an ovenproof casserole dish. Fry the onion and garlic in a little more butter until softened.

2 Add the stout, stock, bay leaves, horseradish sauce and a little seasoning to the frying pan. Bring to the boil and pour the mixture over the meat. Transfer to a preheated oven, 150°C (300°F), Gas Mark 2, and cook for 1½ hours until the meat is tender.

3 Meanwhile, fry the mushrooms in the remaining butter for 5 minutes and add them to the beef for the last 30 minutes. Leave to cool, then turn the meat mixture into a 1 litre (1¾ pint) pie dish and chill.

4 Roll out the pastry until it is 5 cm (2 inches) larger than the dish, and use to cover the pie (see page 25). Bake in a preheated oven, 190°C (375°F), Gas Mark 5, for 45 minutes until deep golden.

Steak and chips with béarnaise sauce

If you're going to indulge in a prime steak, it's worth making a bit of an effort over these 'shoestring' chips.

PREPARATION TIME: 20 minutes

COOKING TIME: 20–30 minutes

SERVES: 4

500 g (1 lb) floury potatoes (e.g., Maris Piper)

4 steaks (e.g., sirloin, fillet, rump or T-bone)

15 g (½ oz) chopped tarragon or chervil

2 shallots, finely chopped

3 tablespoons white wine vinegar

1 teaspoon black peppercorns

3 egg yolks

200 g (7 oz) unsalted butter, cut into cubes, plus 1 tablespoon

vegetable oil, for frying

salt and pepper

1 Cut the potatoes into slices 5 mm (¼ inch) thick, then across into matchstick-sized chips. Put in a bowl with lots of cold water. Season the steaks.

2 Put a quarter of the herbs in a small, saucepan with the shallots, vinegar, peppercorns and 1 tablespoon water. Cook until reduced to 1 tablespoon.

3 Heat a little water in a medium-sized pan until simmering. Put the egg yolks in a heatproof bowl over the pan, making sure the base of the bowl doesn't touch the water. Strain the vinegar mixture into the bowl. Add a cube of butter and whisk into the sauce until melted. Keep adding the butter, a cube at a time, until the sauce is thick and glossy. Stir in the remaining chopped herbs and season to taste. Turn off the heat, cover and leave to stand.

4 Drain the chips and pat them dry on kitchen paper. Heat 8 cm (3½ inches) of oil in a deep fryer or large, heavy-based saucepan until a chip sizzles on the surface. Add half the chips and fry for about 5 minutes until soft but not golden. Drain and fry the remainder.

5 Melt the tablespoon of butter in a frying pan or griddle and fry the steaks, turning once, until cooked to your liking (see page 12). Transfer to warm serving plates.

6 Return all the chips to the hot oil and fry for 2–3 minutes until crisp and golden. Drain thoroughly and serve with the steak and sauce.

Boeuf bourguignon
Although it's not essential, the flavour and texture of a stew are often improved if it's cooked a day or so in advance and then reheated. Serve with plenty of creamy mashed potato to absorb the rich wine sauce.

PREPARATION TIME: 20 minutes, plus marinating

COOKING TIME: about 2 hours

SERVES: 6

1 kg (2 lb) braising steak, cut into chunks

2 onions, chopped

600 ml (1 pint) Burgundy or other full-flavoured red wine

3 garlic cloves, chopped

several sprigs of thyme

25 g (1 oz) butter

175 g (6 oz) smoked bacon lardons

2 tablespoons plain flour

2 tablespoons brandy

375 g (12 oz) baby onions or shallots, peeled

200 g (7 oz) button mushrooms

salt and pepper

chopped flat leaf parsley, to garnish

1 Put the meat, onions, wine, garlic and thyme in a large, non-metallic bowl. Cover and leave overnight in the refrigerator.

2 Drain, reserving the liquid. Remove the pieces of meat and pat them dry on kitchen paper. Use half the butter to fry the meat in small batches until well browned, using a slotted spoon to drain and transfer each batch to a large saucepan.

3 Melt a little more butter and fry the bacon until it is golden. Add the flour and cook, stirring, for 1 minute. Stir in the brandy, strained marinade and seasoning and bring just to the boil. Pour over the meat, cover and cook on the lowest possible heat for about 1½ hours until the meat is tender.

4 Meanwhile, melt the remaining butter in a frying pan and fry the onions, then the mushrooms until they are beginning to brown. Add to the meat for the last 30 minutes. Check the seasoning and serve sprinkled with parsley.

Beef Wellington

Wrapping beef in pâté and pastry is an enduring and delicious way to serve a prime fillet. Serve with new potatoes and a herb salad or, in winter, vegetables and a red wine sauce.

PREPARATION TIME: 30 minutes

COOKING TIME: about 1 hour

SERVES: 6

1.5 kg (3 lb) piece beef fillet (preferably cut from the middle of the fillet)

50 g (2 oz) butter

2 small onions, finely chopped

300 g (10 oz) chestnut mushrooms, chopped

2 tablespoons brandy

500 g (1 lb) puff pastry (thawed if frozen)

200 g (7 oz) smooth chicken pâté

1 egg, lightly beaten

salt and pepper

1 Trim off the excess fat and season the beef. Melt the butter in a frying pan and sear the beef on all sides. Transfer it to a roasting tin, reserving the fat in the pan, and roast in a preheated oven, 200°C (400°F), Gas Mark 6, for 20 minutes. Leave to cool.

2 Fry the onions in the pan for 5 minutes. Add the mushrooms and a little seasoning and fry until the moisture has evaporated. Add the brandy and fry for a further 1 minute. Leave to cool.

3 Thinly roll out the pastry to a large rectangle. Spread the top of the meat with the pâté, then press a thick layer of the mushroom mixture over the top. Invert the beef on to the pastry and spread with the remaining mushrooms.

4 Brush the pastry with beaten egg and bring it up over the fillet to enclose the meat completely, trimming off any bulky areas at the corners. Place, join side down, on a lightly greased baking sheet and brush with more egg. Bake for 35 minutes, until deep golden. Leave to stand for 20 minutes before carving.

Tip

To make a red wine sauce, fry 1 small onion in a little butter, sprinkle in some plain flour and cook for 1 minute. Add 450 ml (¾ pint) beef stock, a large glass of red wine and seasoning. Bubble until reduced by about half.

Fillet of beef with walnuts
Requiring little preparation, this steak recipe is pretty much unbeatable. It can be made ahead, including the gravy, ready for a quick blast in a hot oven before serving.

PREPARATION TIME: 20 minutes

COOKING TIME: 20 minutes

SERVES: 6

50 g (2 oz) butter

3 shallots, finely chopped

3 garlic cloves, crushed

2 teaspoons chopped rosemary

125 g (4 oz) walnut pieces, roughly chopped

125 g (4 oz) pickled walnuts, drained and roughly chopped

1 tablespoon hot horseradish sauce

1 kg (2 lb) piece fillet of beef

1 tablespoon olive oil

300 ml (½ pint) beef, veal or chicken stock

1 large glass of red wine

salt and pepper

chopped flat leaf parsley, to garnish

1 Melt half the butter in a large, heavy-based frying pan and fry the shallots for 3–4 minutes until softened. Stir in the garlic and rosemary, tip the mixture into a bowl and add all the walnuts, the horseradish sauce and a little seasoning.

2 Slice the beef into 6 equal pieces and season. Melt the remaining butter with the oil in the frying pan and sear the steaks on all sides. Transfer to a roasting tin, leaving the frying pan to one side.

3 Pile the walnut mixture on the steaks and press down gently. Transfer to a preheated oven, 200°C (400°F), Gas Mark 6, for 10 minutes.

4 Meanwhile, pour the stock and wine into the pan and bring to the boil, stirring to scrape up any residue. Let the mixture bubble until reduced by about half. Transfer the steaks to warm plates, pour over a little sauce and scatter with parsley. Serve the remaining sauce separately.

Mexican chilli

Although it's not authentically Mexican, chilli con carne is a deliciously spicy bean stew, which benefits from slow and gentle cooking. This version uses diced braising steak, although you can easily substitute lean minced beef. You can either buy this ready prepared or mince it yourself at home.

PREPARATION TIME: 20 minutes, plus soaking

COOKING TIME: 1 hour 40 minutes

SERVES: 6

250 g (8 oz) dried red or black kidney beans
750 g (1½ lb) lean braising steak, diced
3 tablespoons olive oil
2 onions, chopped
1 tablespoon mild chilli powder
1 tablespoon cumin seeds, crushed
1 teaspoon celery salt
3 garlic cloves, crushed
2 tablespoons dark muscovado sugar
1 glass of red wine
150 ml (¼ pint) beef or chicken stock
2 400 g (13 oz) cans chopped tomatoes
salt and pepper
crème fraîche, to serve
chopped coriander, to garnish

1 Cover the beans with cold water and leave to soak overnight. Drain and put them in a large saucepan with fresh water. Bring to the boil and boil rapidly for 10 minutes. Drain and reserve.

2 Season the steak. Heat the oil in a large, heavy-based saucepan and fry the beef in 2 batches until well browned. Drain and remove from the pan.

3 Add the onions to the pan with the chilli powder, cumin seeds and celery salt and fry gently for 5 minutes. Add the garlic and sugar and fry for 1 minute.

4 Return the beef to the pan with the wine, stock, tomatoes and beans. Bubble, then reduce the heat and simmer, covered, for 1¼ hours until the meat is tender. Serve with crème fraîche and coriander.

Swedish meatballs

Coated in a sweet, spicy cranberry glaze, these bite-sized meatballs make a good family supper dish with pappardelle or tagliatelle. Mixing the meat and flavourings in a food processor gives the meatballs their characteristic smooth texture.

PREPARATION TIME: 20 minutes

COOKING TIME: about 30 minutes

SERVES: 4

300 g (10 oz) lean veal mince

200 g (7 oz) lean pork mince

1 small onion, chopped

1 garlic clove, crushed

25 g (1 oz) breadcrumbs

1 egg yolk

3 tablespoons chopped flat leaf parsley

2 tablespoons vegetable oil

salt and pepper

Cranberry glaze

150 g (5 oz) good-quality cranberry sauce

100 ml (3½ fl oz) chicken or vegetable stock

2 tablespoons sweet chilli sauce

1 tablespoon lemon juice

1 Make the cranberry glaze. Combine the cranberry sauce, stock, chilli sauce and lemon juice in a small pan and heat gently until smooth. Leave to simmer gently for 5 minutes.

2 Put the veal and pork mince in a food processor with the onion, garlic, breadcrumbs, egg yolk, parsley and a little seasoning and blend until the mixture forms a fairly smooth paste that clings together.

3 Scoop teaspoonfuls of the paste and roll them into small balls between the palms of your hands.

4 Heat the oil in a large, heavy-based frying pan and fry half the meatballs for 8–10 minutes until golden. Drain and fry the remainder. Return all the meatballs to the pan and add the cranberry glaze. Cook gently for 2–3 minutes until very hot. Serve immediately.

Spice-crusted burgers with crème fraîche

Making burgers from scratch enables you to throw in additional flavours, such as chopped herbs, garlic or spices. For the tenderest texture make the mince yourself (see page 9).

PREPARATION TIME: 15 minutes

COOKING TIME: 12 minutes

SERVES: 4

½ teaspoon crushed black pepper

2 teaspoons cumin seeds, lightly crushed

2 teaspoons coriander seeds, lightly crushed

500 g (1 lb) minced beef

2 shallots, finely chopped

4 tablespoons olive or vegetable oil

150 ml (¼ pint) crème fraîche

salt

1 Mix together the pepper, cumin and coriander seeds and set them aside.

2 Put the minced beef in a bowl with the shallots and a little salt and mix together well. (This is most easily done with your hands.) Divide the mixture into 4 equal portions and shape each into a burger. Sprinkle the spice mixture over both sides of each burger and press in gently.

3 Heat the oil in a large, heavy-based frying pan and gently fry the burgers for 4–5 minutes on each side if you want them slightly pink in the centre. Cook for a few minutes extra if you prefer them well done.

4 Drain the burgers and keep them warm. Add 3 tablespoons water and the crème fraîche to the pan and cook until bubbling, scraping up the residue from the sides of the pan. Pour the sauce over the burgers and serve.

Tip

This recipe is finished with a delicious crème fraîche sauce, but omit this if you're serving the burgers in buns and add your favourite sauce or salsa instead.

Steak meatloaf

Serve this meatloaf hot or cold, depending on the weather and circumstances. Leftovers, accompanied with salad and chutney, make an ideal lunchtime snack.

PREPARATION TIME: 30 minutes

COOKING TIME: 2½ hours

SERVES: 6

2 red peppers, deseeded and cut into chunks

1 red onion, sliced

3 tablespoons olive oil

300 g (10 oz) thin-cut streaky bacon

500 g (1 lb) lean steak mince

250 g (8 oz) pork mince

2 tablespoons chopped oregano

2 tablespoons chopped flat leaf parsley

3 tablespoons Worcestershire sauce

2 tablespoons sun-dried tomato paste

50 g (2 oz) breadcrumbs

1 egg

salt and pepper

1 Scatter the peppers and onion in a roasting tin and drizzle with the oil. Cook in a preheated oven, 200°C (400°F), Gas Mark 6, for 30 minutes until lightly roasted, then chop. Reduce the heat to 160°C (325°F), Gas Mark 3.

2 Use some bacon to line the base and long sides of a 1 kg (2 lb) loaf tin, overlapping them slightly and letting the ends overhang the sides. Finely chop the rest.

3 Mix together both minces, the chopped bacon, roasted vegetables, herbs, Worcestershire sauce, tomato paste, breadcrumbs, egg and seasoning.

4 Pack the mixture into the tin and fold the ends of the bacon over the filling. Cover with foil, place in a roasting tin and pour in 2 cm (¾ inch) boiling water. Cook in the oven for 2 hours.

5 To serve hot, leave for 15 minutes, then invert on to a serving plate. To serve cold, cool in the tin, remove and wrap in foil.

Steak meatloaf

Salt beef in cider

You can order salt beef from a butcher but it's more satisfying to salt and cook your own. This version can be served hot with its cooking juices, creamy mash, mustard and gherkins, or chilled for cold meat platters or sandwiches. Once cooked, it'll keep in the refrigerator for up to a week.

PREPARATION TIME: 15 minutes, plus 8 days marinating and soaking

COOKING TIME: 2–2½ hours

SERVES: 6–8

1.75 kg (3½ lb) piece brisket of beef

2 large carrots, chopped

1 onion, chopped

900 ml (1½ pints) medium cider

Brine

250 g (8 oz) dark muscovado sugar

675 g (1 lb 6 oz) sea salt

1 teaspoon black peppercorns

2 teaspoons juniper berries, crushed

2 teaspoons allspice berries

1 teaspoon crushed blade mace

several sprigs of thyme

1 Make the brine. Put the sugar, salt, peppercorns, juniper and allspice berries, mace and thyme in a large saucepan with 2.5 litres (4 pints) water and heat until the sugar has dissolved. Bring to the boil and cook for 2 minutes. Leave to cool.

2 Put the beef in a non-metallic container (a large glass mixing bowl or plastic container is ideal). Add the brine, making sure the meat is completely covered. If necessary, use a plate or lid to keep the meat submerged. Leave to marinate in the refrigerator for 1 week.

3 Drain the meat and soak in cold water for a further 24 hours, changing the water once or twice to remove excess salt.

4 Drain the meat and put it in a casserole dish into which it fits quite snugly. Add the carrots, onion and cider and top up with enough boiling water to just cover the meat. Cover with a lid and cook in a preheated oven, 120°C (250°F), Gas Mark ½, for 2–2½ hours or until the meat is tender. Drain and serve hot or leave to cool in the liquid.

Variations

Beef silverside or a whole tongue can be cooked in the same way. If you use tongue increase the cooking time if necessary, so that it is completely tender when pierced with a knife. Remove the skin before serving.

Seared carpaccio of beef

This fabulous dish showcases the delicious flavour and succulence of a prime piece of sirloin or, if you prefer, thick end of fillet. Carve as thinly as possible and arrange the slices on a large platter for an impressive starter or summer lunch, served with crusty bread.

PREPARATION TIME: 15 minutes, plus standing

COOKING TIME: 5 minutes

SERVES: 6

1 kg (2 lb) beef sirloin or fillet

2 teaspoons finely chopped thyme

100 ml (3½ fl oz) extra virgin olive oil

1–2 tablespoons white wine vinegar

1 tablespoon finely grated fresh horseradish
   or 1 tablespoon hot horseradish sauce

½ teaspoon caster sugar

10–12 radishes

50 g (2 oz) rocket leaves

salt and pepper

1 Trim any fat from the meat. Mix the thyme with plenty of salt and pepper and rub it into the surface of the meat.

2 Heat a dash of the oil in a heavy-based frying pan and sear the meat on all sides until deep golden, which will take about 5 minutes. Drain the meat, transfer it to a board and leave to stand for 10 minutes.

3 Use a very sharp knife to slice the meat as thinly as possible and arrange the slices on a large platter.

4 Beat the remaining oil with 1 tablespoon of the vinegar, the horseradish, sugar and a little seasoning. Add a little extra vinegar if the dressing tastes bland. Slice the radishes as finely as possible and scatter over the meat with the rocket. Drizzle with the dressing and serve.

Fillet of beef teriyaki
Tender lean beef fillet is perfect for absorbing strong, aromatic flavours like soy sauce and ginger. It's a good lightweight alternative to more substantial roast meat.

PREPARATION TIME: 15 minutes, plus marinating

COOKING TIME: 20 minutes

SERVES: 4

500 g (1 lb) beef fillet

2 tablespoons sesame oil

4 tablespoons light soy sauce

2 tablespoons rice wine vinegar

1 tablespoon clear honey

1 teaspoon five-spice powder

1 small garlic clove, crushed

1 pointed red pepper

1 bunch spring onions

200 g (7 oz) pak choi, roughly shredded

25 g (1 oz) pickled ginger, shredded

1 tablespoon sesame seeds, lightly toasted

1 Cut away any pieces of fat from the meat, then pat it dry and put it in a small roasting tin. Brush with 1 tablespoon of the oil and roast in a preheated oven, 220°C (425°F), Gas Mark 7, for 20 minutes.

2 Mix together the soy sauce, vinegar, honey, five-spice, garlic and remaining oil.

3 Transfer the cooked meat to a shallow dish. While still hot, spoon over the soy sauce mixture. Leave to cool, turning the meat in the marinade, then cover and chill for several hours or overnight.

4 Spear the pepper with a fork and hold over the flame or heated ring of the hob, turning it until the skin chars. Cover with clingfilm for 5 minutes then peel away the skin. Halve and deseed the pepper and finely shred the flesh. Trim the spring onions, cut them in half, then quarter them lengthways. Blanch the spring onions and pak choi in boiling water for 30 seconds. Drain well.

5 Mix the vegetables with the pepper and ginger and pile them on to serving plates. Thinly slice the beef, arrange on top and spoon over the marinade. Scatter with the sesame seeds.

Malaysian beef and aubergine curry
This quick and easy curry is packed with hot spices in a creamy coconut sauce. If you prefer a milder flavour halve the quantity of crushed chillies when you're grinding the spices.

PREPARATION TIME: 20 minutes

COOKING TIME: about 1¾ hours

SERVES: 4–5

2 teaspoons cumin seeds

2 teaspoons coriander seeds

1 cinnamon stick

½ teaspoon crushed dried chillies

6 cloves

300 g (10 oz) aubergines

1 kg (2 lb) lean braising beef

5 tablespoons vegetable oil

2 large onions, sliced

1 tablespoon tamarind paste

2 tablespoons dark muscovado sugar

150 ml (¼ pint) coconut cream

salt

1 Put the cumin, coriander, cinnamon, dried chillies and cloves in a small food processor or completely clean coffee grinder and grind as finely as possible.

2 Cut the aubergines into 2 cm (¾ inch) cubes. Discard any excess fat from the beef and cut the meat into chunks.

3 Heat the oil in a large, heavy-based frying pan and fry the onions for 6–8 minutes until lightly browned. Add the blended spices and fry, stirring, for 1 minute. Add the beef and fry, stirring, for 2–3 minutes until the meat is coated in the spices.

4 Add 400 ml (14 fl oz) water, the tamarind paste and sugar and bring just to the boil. Cover with a lid and cook over the lowest heat for 1 hour or until the meat is tender.

5 Stir in the coconut cream and aubergines, cover and cook for a further 20–30 minutes until the aubergines are soft. Check the seasoning and serve.

Beef and noodle broth

This quick and easy soup relies on good well-flavoured stock and is ideal for using up any beef or chicken stock that you might have in the freezer. When slicing the beef, use a sharp knife and cut it across the grain, so that it falls into tender, succulent slices.

PREPARATION TIME: 15 minutes

COOKING TIME: 10 minutes

SERVES: 2

300 g (10 oz) rump or sirloin steak

15 g (½ oz) fresh root ginger, grated

2 teaspoons soy sauce

50 g (2 oz) vermicelli rice noodles

600 ml (1 pint) beef or chicken stock

1 red chilli, deseeded and finely chopped

1 garlic clove, thinly sliced

2 teaspoons caster sugar

2 teaspoons vegetable oil

75 g (3 oz) sugar snap peas, halved lengthways

small handful Thai basil, torn into pieces

1 Trim any fat from the beef. Mix the ginger with 1 teaspoon of the soy sauce and smooth over both sides of the beef.

2 Cook the noodles according to the directions on the packet. Drain and rinse thoroughly in cold water.

3 Bring the stock to a gentle simmer with the chilli, garlic and sugar. Cover and cook gently for 5 minutes.

4 Heat the oil in a small, heavy-based frying pan and fry the beef for 2 minutes on each side. Transfer the meat to a board, cut it in half lengthways and then cut it across into thin strips.

5 Add the noodles, peas, basil and remaining soy sauce to the soup and heat gently for 1 minute. Stir in the beef and serve immediately.

Beef and noodle broth

Oxtail stew
Oxtail is best served quite simply with plenty of vegetables in a beefy, beery stock. This is definitely a dish for cooking in advance so you can chill it, lift off the fat and reheat until the meat's lovely and tender.

PREPARATION TIME: 20 minutes

COOKING TIME: 2¾ hours

SERVES: 4

2 tablespoons plain flour

1.5 kg (3 lb) oxtail, cut into thick slices

3 tablespoons oil

2 onions, chopped

500 g (1 lb) carrots, chunkily sliced

2 celery sticks, sliced

several sprigs of thyme

2 tablespoons tomato paste

300 ml (½ pint) beer

300 ml (½ pint) beef stock

salt and pepper

1 Season the flour and use it to coat the oxtail. Heat 2 tablespoons of the oil in a large, heavy-based frying pan and fry the meat, in batches, until browned. Drain and transfer to an ovenproof casserole dish.

2 Add the remaining oil to the pan and fry the vegetables for 5 minutes until softened.

3 Stir in the thyme, tomato paste, beer, stock and a little seasoning and bring just to the boil. Pour the vegetable mixture over the meat and cover with a lid.

4 Cook in a preheated oven, 160°C (325°F), Gas Mark 3, for 2½ hours or until the meat is tender. Leave to cool, then chill overnight.

5 The next day skim off the layer of fat and reheat the stew in the oven for about 1 hour before serving.

Calf's liver and bacon
Calf's liver is the prime choice for pan-frying with bacon, although lamb's liver is a good substitute. Fry the liver a little longer if you prefer it cooked through but take care not to cook it for too long or it will start to toughen up.

PREPARATION TIME: 10 minutes

COOKING TIME: 6–8 minutes

SERVES: 4

2 teaspoons plain flour

625 g (1¼ lb) calf's liver

25 g (1 oz) butter

1 tablespoon olive oil

12 large sage leaves

8 rashers of back bacon

150 ml (¼ pint) dry cider

salt and pepper

1 Season the flour. Cut away any tubes from the liver and dust it with the flour.

2 Melt half the butter with the oil in a large frying pan until bubbling. Add the sage leaves and cook for about 30 seconds until sizzling. Drain and transfer them to a plate with a slotted spoon.

3 Fry the bacon until golden, drain and transfer to the plate and keep warm. Add the liver to the pan and fry for about 2 minutes until deep golden. Turn the slices and return the bacon and sage to the pan. Cook for a further 1–2 minutes. (At this stage the liver will be slightly pink in the centre but cook a little more if preferred.) Drain and keep warm.

4 Add the cider to the pan and let it bubble until slightly reduced, scraping up any residue. Whisk in the remaining butter and check the seasoning. Spoon the sauce over the liver and bacon on serving plates and scatter with the sage leaves.

Vitello tonnato

This veal dish, a speciality of northern Italy, is expensive but well worth it for special summer entertaining. Served cold, both meat and sauce can be prepared the day before they're needed so they're ready for assembling at the last minute. Keep the sauce, covered, in a small dish.

PREPARATION TIME: 20 minutes

COOKING TIME: 1 hour

SERVES: 6

1.25 kg (2½ lb) boned and rolled best end or loin of veal

several sprigs of rosemary

6–8 bay leaves

3 tablespoons olive oil

300 ml (½ pint) dry white wine

salt and pepper

1 tablespoon capers, rinsed and drained, to serve

chopped flat leaf parsley, to garnish

Sauce

75 g (3 oz) can tuna, drained

4 anchovy fillets

2 egg yolks

juice of 1 lemon

150 ml (¼ pint) olive oil

1 Season the veal with salt and pepper and push the rosemary and bay leaves under the string tying the veal.

2 Heat the oil in a large, heavy-based frying pan and fry the veal on all sides until it is well browned.

3 Drain and transfer the meat to a casserole dish into which it fits quite snugly and add the wine and any juices from the pan. Cover and cook in a preheated oven, 180°C (350°F), Gas Mark 4, for 1 hour or until the veal is tender, turning the meat once during cooking. Leave to cool in the juices then cover and chill.

4 Make the sauce. Put the tuna, anchovy fillets, egg yolks and 1 tablespoon of the lemon juice in a food processor or blender and blend until smooth. With the machine running, gradually blend in the oil in a thin stream until the mixture has the consistency of pouring cream. Check the seasoning and add a little more lemon juice if necessary for extra tang.

5 To serve, arrange thin slices of the veal on a serving platter. Spoon over the sauce and serve scattered with the capers and parsley.

Osso bucco with gremolata

Osso buco means 'bone and hole' and refers to the thick marrow bone that runs through the centre of the veal shin. The marrow turns soft and creamy during cooking and should be scooped out with a spoon. Serve osso bucco on its own in bowls or with a saffron risotto.

PREPARATION TIME: 20 minutes

COOKING TIME: 2¼ hours

SERVES: 4

1 tablespoon plain flour

4 thick slices shin of veal

4 tablespoons olive oil

2 carrots, finely chopped

2 onions, finely chopped

300 ml (½ pint) white wine

6 tomatoes, skinned and chopped

3 tablespoons sun-dried tomato paste

300 ml (½ pint) veal or chicken stock

salt and pepper

Gremolata

1 garlic clove, crushed

finely grated rind of 1 lemon

4 tablespoons chopped flat leaf parsley

1 Season the flour and use it to coat the veal. Heat the oil in a large, heavy-based frying pan and fry the veal on both sides until it is thoroughly browned. Drain and transfer to a casserole dish.

2 Add the carrots and onions to the frying pan and fry gently for 5–10 minutes until softened. Stir in the wine and bring to the boil.

3 Add the vegetable mixture to the veal, with the tomatoes, tomato paste and stock. Cover and cook in a preheated oven, 160°C (325°F), Gas Mark 3, for 2 hours or until the veal is tender and beginning to come away from the bone.

4 Meanwhile, make the gremolata. Mix the garlic, lemon rind and parsley.

5 Use a fish slice to remove the meat from the casserole and keep it warm. Tip the tomato mixture into a pan and bring to the boil. Cook for 6–8 minutes until thickened. Spoon over the meat and serve, scattered with the gremolata.

Veal saltimbocca

Several Italian dishes use veal escalopes as a base. Bashed thin, they're quick to cook and stay moist and tender. This recipe is easy enough for the 'not-so-keen cook' and produces delicious results every time. The quantities can be halved easily if you are cooking for only two.

PREPARATION TIME: 10 minutes

COOKING TIME: 10 minutes

SERVES: 4

8 small veal escalopes
2 teaspoons plain flour
50 g (2 oz) butter
8 slices of prosciutto
8 large sage leaves
250 ml (8 fl oz) dry white wine
salt and pepper

1 Place the veal escalopes between 2 layers of clingfilm and beat them with a rolling pin or meat mallet until they are very thin. Season the flour and use it to dust the meat.

2 Melt 25 g (1 oz) of the butter in a large, heavy-based frying pan and quickly fry the veal, in batches, until lightly browned, draining the meat and transferring the slices to a plate.

3 Lay a slice of prosciutto and 1 sage leaf on the centre of each escalope and return them to the pan for a further 2–3 minutes until cooked through, carefully turning each escalope once to sear the prosciutto and sage. Drain and transfer to warm serving plates.

4 Pour the wine into the pan and let it bubble until reduced by about half. Cut the remaining butter into pieces and whisk into the wine. Season to taste and pour the sauce over the escalopes to serve.

Veal saltimbocca

Lamb *This is the sweetest of all meats and the one that has suffered least from intensive farming. Its flavour depends very much on its feed, region of farming, hanging time and age at slaughter. Winter reared 'spring lamb' is fattened up quickly for the Easter market but lacks the flavour and succulence of lamb that has been given time to graze through the summer months. Inevitably this makes late summer to autumn the best time for buying.*

Lean, roasted lamb has a better texture and flavour if cooked fast and 'pink' in the centre, while cheaper, fattier cuts make superb, slow cooked stews and casseroles. These often benefit from 'twice cooking' – cooking and cooling the dish so that the fat layer can be skimmed off before reheating.

Mediterranean roast lamb

Using a boned leg of lamb makes carving easier and lets the flavours of the stuffing penetrate the meat. This recipe gives a slightly pink result, so part cook the lamb at the lower temperature for 30 minutes before adding the potatoes if you prefer it well done.

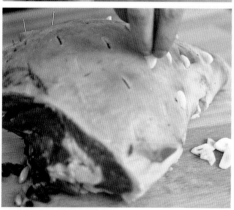

PREPARATION TIME: 25 minutes

COOKING TIME: 2¼ hours

SERVES: 6

50 g (2 oz) sun-dried tomatoes in oil, drained

100 g (3½ oz) grilled aubergines in oil, drained

7 tablespoons olive oil

2 red onions, chopped

6 garlic cloves, thinly sliced

75 g (3 oz) pine nuts

1 leg of lamb, about 1.5 kg (3 lb), part boned

1.5 kg (3 lb) large potatoes, cut into 2 cm (¾ inch) chunks

1 tablespoon chopped rosemary

300 ml (½ pint) lamb stock or white wine

salt and pepper

1 Finely chop the tomatoes and aubergines. Heat 2 tablespoons of oil in a frying pan and fry 1 onion until soft. Add the vegetables (not the potatoes), half the garlic, half the pine nuts and seasoning. Stuff the lamb, skewer the end to close.

2 Blanch the potatoes in boiling, salted water for 5 minutes. Mix the remaining chopped onion, rosemary and remaining pine nuts with the rest of the oil. Toss with the potatoes and seasoning.

3 Make small incisions over the lamb and insert a garlic slice into each. Roast the meat in a preheated oven, 220°C (425°F), Gas Mark 7, for 30 minutes. Surround with the potato mixture, reduce the heat to 160°C (325°F), Gas Mark 3, and cook for 1¼ hours, turning the potatoes once.

4 Drain and transfer to a serving platter. Add the stock or wine to the pan. Boil, scraping up the residue, season then serve.

Mediterranean roast lamb

Harissa lamb in a salt crust
Cooking a joint of meat under a blanket of salt dough has the same effect as using a lid – it keeps the meat amazingly moist and succulent.

PREPARATION TIME: 25 minutes

COOKING TIME: 1¼ hours

SERVES: 6

6 small heads garlic, plus 6 crushed cloves

4 teaspoons chopped rosemary

4 tablespoons chopped parsley

1 tablespoon harissa paste

1.75 kg (3½ lb) leg of lamb

5 red peppers, deseeded and chopped into chunks

400 g (13 oz) tomatoes, skinned and roughly chopped

1 red onion, chopped

4 tablespoons olive oil

salt and pepper

Salt crust

300 g (10 oz) plain flour

200 g (7 oz) table salt

200 ml (7 fl oz) cold water

1 Mix the crushed garlic with the rosemary, parsley, harissa paste and a little seasoning and rub it over the lamb. Place in a roasting tin. Slice the tops off the garlic heads. Put the red peppers, tomatoes, onion and olive oil in a separate tin.

2 Make the salt crust. Mix the flour and salt in a bowl and stir in the water to make a firm dough. Leave to stand for 10 minutes then roll out the dough to an oval, about 10 cm (4 inches) longer and wider than the lamb. Lift the dough over the meat and fit it around the sides so that the meat is completely covered.

3 Roast in a preheated oven, 200°C (400°F), Gas Mark 6, for 1¼ hours, adding the garlic heads to the tin. Move the tin containing peppers and tomatoes above the lamb after 20 minutes.

4 Transfer the lamb to a platter, pouring the pan juices into a small jug, and leave to stand for 15 minutes. Blend the pepper mixture in a food processor until roughly pulped. Turn into a serving dish.

5 Break open the crust with a knife and discard it. Carve the lamb and serve with the roasted garlic, pepper and tomato sauce.

Lamb and leek stew with rosemary dumplings

Although very fatty, breast of lamb has a delicious, sweet flavour and is well worth using in an inexpensive stew. Make the stew a day in advance so that you can chill it overnight, then lift off the fat before heating it through with its topping of fluffy hot dumplings.

PREPARATION TIME: 25 minutes, plus chilling

COOKING TIME: 1¾ hours

SERVES: 4

875 g (1¾ lb) breast of lamb

2 tablespoons vegetable oil

1 onion, chopped

400 g (13 oz) carrots, sliced

2 celery sticks, sliced

3 bay leaves

75 g (3 oz) pearl barley

425 g (14 oz) small leeks, sliced

salt and pepper

Dumplings

150 g (5 oz) self-raising flour

75 g (3 oz) beef or vegetable suet

2 teaspoons chopped rosemary

125 ml (4 fl oz) water

1 Cut the lamb into chunks. Heat 1 tablespoon of the oil in a large, heavy-based frying pan and fry the lamb until it is well browned. Drain and transfer to a large saucepan.

2 Drain the excess fat from the pan and fry the onion for 5 minutes. Add the carrots, celery, bay leaves and 1.5 litres (2½ pints) water. Bring to the boil and pour over the lamb. Stir in the pearl barley and a little seasoning and bring to a gentle simmer. Cover with a lid and cook on the lowest possible heat for about 1 hour until the lamb is tender.

3 Meanwhile, fry the leeks in the remaining oil and add them to the stew. Cook for a further 15 minutes, leave to cool, then tip into a bowl and chill overnight.

4 Make the dumplings. Mix together the flour, suet and rosemary with a little salt and add the water to make a firm paste. Remove the layer of fat from the stew, return the stew to the pan and bring it slowly to a simmer.

5 Use a dessertspoon to place 8 scoops of the dumpling paste over the stew, cover and simmer gently until the dumplings are light and fluffy. Serve the stew in shallow bowls.

Lamb with salmoriglio sauce

With their lemony, garlicky, herby sauce these lamb chops are made for alfresco dining and show how an unfussy meal can be really special. Make the salmoriglio sauce several hours in advance so that the flavours have a chance to mingle.

PREPARATION TIME: 10 minutes

COOKING TIME: 15 minutes

SERVES: 4

8 loin of lamb chops or 4 large chump chops

1 tablespoon chopped fresh oregano

2 tablespoons chopped flat leaf parsley

1 tablespoon capers, drained, rinsed and chopped

1 teaspoon dried oregano

3 garlic cloves, crushed

finely grated rind and juice of 1 small lemon

150 ml (¼ pint) extra virgin olive oil

salt and pepper

1 Trim any excess fat from the chops. If using loin chops, tie each chop into a neat shape with string.

2 Mix the chopped oregano with the parsley and capers on a board and put them in a bowl with the dried oregano, garlic, lemon rind and juice, oil and seasoning. Whisk well until combined.

3 Lightly brush a ridged pan with oil and preheat, or set the grill to its highest setting. Cook the chops for 6–7 minutes on each side, brushing halfway through cooking with a little of the sauce. Serve with the remaining sauce.

Lamb with salmoriglio sauce

Slow-cooked aromatic lamb

A good weekend meal if you've got friends staying but don't want to be tied to the kitchen as the meat cooks slowly and gently and doesn't spoil if cooked a little over the stated time. The vegetables can be roasted in advance ready for adding to the meat to reheat.

PREPARATION TIME: 25 minutes, plus marinating

COOKING TIME: about 3 hours

SERVES: 6

1.5 kg (3 lb) boned and rolled shoulder of lamb, or leg

1 onion, cut into quarters

1 orange, cut into wedges with the skin

small handful each of thyme and rosemary sprigs

about 500 ml (17 fl oz) red wine

400 g (13 oz) small carrots

400 g (13 oz) turnips

400 g (13 oz) parsnips

4 tablespoons olive oil

1 head garlic

6 large open mushrooms

salt and pepper

1 Put the lamb in a non-metallic dish into which it fits quite snugly. Tuck the onion quarters, orange wedges and herbs around the meat and pour over the wine. Cover and leave to marinate for about 24 hours, turning once.

2 Peel the carrots, turnips and parsnips and cut each into 3–4 chunks. Put them in a roasting tin and drizzle with 3 tablespoons of the oil. Roast in a preheated oven, 200°C (400°F), Gas Mark 6, for 20 minutes. Cut a slice off the top of the garlic and add it to the tin with the mushrooms. Roast for a further 25 minutes or until the garlic is tender. Reduce the heat to 160°C (325°F), Gas Mark 3.

3 Drain the lamb, reserving the marinade, and pat it dry on kitchen paper. Heat the remaining oil in a roasting tin and thoroughly brown the meat on all sides. Strain the marinade over the lamb. Bring to the boil then cover tightly with foil and bake in the oven for 2 hours.

4 Squeeze the garlic pulp into the cooking juices and tip in the vegetables. Season to taste and return to the oven for a further 20 minutes. Leave to stand for 20 minutes before serving.

Garlic and pine nut crusted lamb

A rack of lamb cooks so quickly and effortlessly that it's a great choice for entertaining. You can get ahead by smothering the lamb in its garlicky crust and leaving it in the refrigerator for the day, covered with clingfilm so the strong flavours are not absorbed into other foods.

PREPARATION TIME: 15 minutes

COOKING TIME: 40 minutes

SERVES: 4–6

2 French-trimmed racks of lamb (see page 15), each about 550 g (1 lb 2 oz)

4 garlic cloves, crushed

1 tablespoon grainy mustard

25 g (1 oz) pine nuts, chopped

2 shallots, finely chopped

4 tablespoons pesto

300 ml (½ pint) lamb stock

1 tablespoon balsamic vinegar

salt and pepper

1 Arrange the racks of lamb, flesh side up, in a roasting tin.

2 Mix the garlic with the mustard, pine nuts, shallots, pesto and a little seasoning and spread the mixture thinly over the surface of the lamb.

3 Roast in a preheated oven, 200°C (400°F), Gas Mark 6, for 25 minutes. (This will give cutlets that are still pink in the middle, so if you prefer them cooked through, cook for an extra 10 minutes.)

4 Transfer the lamb to a platter and leave to stand for 15 minutes. Add the stock and balsamic vinegar to the roasting tin and bring to the boil, scraping up the residue. Boil for about 5 minutes until the sauce is slightly reduced before serving with the lamb.

Rack of lamb with pineapple salsa

The tangy pineapple salsa gives this lamb dish a fresh summery flavour, that's lovely served with steamed couscous or bulgar wheat. Use a very ripe pineapple, which is more likely to be sweet and tender. An underripe fruit will improve in flavour if it's left in the fruit bowl for a few days.

PREPARATION TIME: 10 minutes

COOKING TIME: 8 minutes

SERVES: 4

2 teaspoons chopped thyme

2 French-trimmed racks of lamb (see page 15), about 550 g (1 lb 2 oz) each

½ small pineapple

finely grated rind and juice of 1 lime

2 teaspoons golden caster sugar

1 spring onion, finely chopped

1 large, mild chilli, deseeded and sliced

3 tablespoons roughly chopped coriander

salt and pepper

1 Mix the thyme with plenty of salt and pepper and rub over the surface of the lamb racks. Fit the two racks together so the bones interlock and place in a roasting tin. Roast in a preheated oven, 200°C (400°F), Gas Mark 6, for 25 minutes. Cover and leave to stand for 15 minutes while making the salsa.

2 Cut away the skin and core from the pineapple and finely chop the flesh.

3 Mix the lime rind and juice in a bowl with the sugar until the sugar dissolves. Tip in the pineapple, spring onion, chilli, coriander and a little salt and mix together. Turn into a small serving dish.

4 To carve the lamb, transfer to a plate or board and separate the racks. Cut into single or double cutlets between the ribs. Arrange on warmed serving plates and serve with the salsa.

Rack of lamb with pineapple salsa

Aromatic barbecued lamb

This recipe can also be made with lamb chops, allowing two or three per person. Chump chops are ideal, however, as they have a good proportion of fat, which helps keep the meat deliciously moist and succulent during cooking. Serve with baked potatoes and a cucumber and spring onion salad.

PREPARATION TIME: 10 minutes

COOKING TIME: 8–16 minutes

SERVES: 4

4 lamb chump chops

15 g (½ oz) fresh root ginger, grated

2 garlic cloves, crushed

1 red chilli, deseeded and thinly sliced

2 teaspoons dark muscovado sugar

3 tablespoons soy sauce

2 tablespoons dry sherry

1 Place the lamb chops in a shallow, non-metallic dish. Mix the ginger with the garlic, chilli, sugar, soy sauce and sherry and pour it over the lamb.

2 Turn the meat in the mixture, cover and chill for at least 2 hours or overnight.

3 Barbecue the lamb for 3–8 minutes on each side, depending on whether you like the meat rare or well done. (Alternatively, you could use a griddle or grill.) Use any excess marinade to baste the meat while it is cooking.

Navarin of lamb
This French country stew is great at any time of year but particularly in spring, when all the new season vegetables are available.

PREPARATION TIME: 25 minutes

COOKING TIME: about 2 hours

SERVES: 6

1.5 kg (3 lb) boned shoulder of lamb

2 tablespoons plain flour

50 g (2 oz) butter

1 tablespoon olive oil

1 tablespoon caster sugar

1 large onion, chopped

2 celery sticks, chopped

1 litre (1¾ pints) lamb or vegetable stock

3 garlic cloves, crushed

1 teaspoon chopped rosemary or thyme

3 tablespoons tomato paste

300 g (10 oz) baby carrots

300 g (10 oz) baby turnips

500 g (1 lb) baby potatoes

300 g (10 oz) French beans

100 g (3½ oz) shelled peas

salt and pepper

1 Cut the lamb into small chunks and discard any excess fat. Season the flour and use it to coat the lamb. Melt 25 g (1 oz) of the butter with the oil in a large, heavy-based frying pan and fry the lamb, in batches, until it is golden, adding a little sugar to each batch when frying. Turn the meat into a casserole dish.

2 Add the onion and celery to the frying pan and fry gently for 5 minutes. Stir in the stock, garlic, herbs and tomato paste and bring to the boil, stirring to scrape up the pan juices. Pour the mixture over the meat, cover with a lid and bake in a preheated oven, 150°C (300°C), Gas Mark 2, for 1½ hours until tender.

3 Meanwhile, trim the carrots and turnips. Melt the remaining butter in the frying pan and sauté the carrots, turnips and potatoes, turning them frequently, until softened. Blanch the beans and peas in boiling water for 2 minutes.

4 Add all the vegetables to the stew and cook for a further 20 minutes or until tender. Check the seasoning and serve.

Indian lamb with almond sauce
This recipe is like a quick and easy roghan josh with chunks of tender lamb in a richly spiced, nutty sauce. Like many spiced meat dishes, this reheats well.

PREPARATION TIME: 25 minutes

COOKING TIME: 1¼ hours

SERVES: 5–6

750 g (1½ lb) lamb neck fillet

10 whole cardamom pods

1 tablespoon cumin seeds

3 tablespoons vegetable oil

1 hot red chilli, deseeded and chopped

1 tablespoon desiccated coconut

50 g (2 oz) blanched almonds, chopped

40 g (1½ oz) fresh root ginger, grated

4 garlic cloves, chopped

1 teaspoon ground turmeric

1 onion, finely chopped

4 tablespoons natural yogurt

500 g (1 lb) tomatoes, skinned and chopped

salt

1 Cut the lamb into chunks, discarding any fat, and pat dry. Crush the cardamom and cumin seeds. Heat the oil in a large, heavy-based frying pan and gently fry the chilli, cardamom and cumin.

2 Add half the lamb and fry, stirring, until well browned. Drain and transfer the meat to a large saucepan. Fry the remaining lamb and add it to the pan.

3 Add the coconut and almonds to the frying pan and fry until lightly browned. Tip into a blender or food processor with the ginger, garlic, turmeric, onion and 6 tablespoons water and blend to a paste. Return to the frying pan, add the yogurt and cook, stirring, for 5 minutes.

4 Stir in another 150 ml (¼ pint) water and pour over the lamb. Add the tomatoes. Cover and cook on the lowest heat for about 1 hour or until the lamb is tender. Season to taste and serve with rice.

Indian lamb with almond sauce

Moroccan saffron lamb
Any fairly lean, diced lamb, such as neck fillet or a boned shoulder, will give excellent results in this spicy stew. Serve with steamed couscous, flavoured with toasted almonds or pine nuts, melted butter and lemon juice.

PREPARATION TIME: 20 minutes

COOKING TIME: about 1 hour

SERVES: 4

½ teaspoon saffron strands, lightly crushed

1 tablespoon plain flour

500 g (1 lb) lamb, diced

4 tablespoons olive oil

1 large onion, chopped

3 garlic cloves, crushed

1 cinnamon stick

5 cm (2 inch) fresh root ginger, grated

450 ml (¾ pint) lamb or chicken stock

400 g (13 oz) can chickpeas, drained

75 g (3 oz) ready-to-eat dried apricots, chopped

500 g (1 lb) pumpkin, skinned and cut into small chunks

salt and pepper

fresh chopped coriander, to garnish

1 Sprinkle the saffron over 1 tablespoon boiling water in a small bowl. Season the flour and use it to coat the lamb.

2 Heat the oil in a large, heavy-based saucepan and fry the onion and garlic for 3 minutes. Use a slotted spoon to drain and transfer the onion and garlic to another dish, and fry the lamb, in batches, for 5 minutes or until lightly browned. Return the onions and garlic, add the cinnamon, ginger and stock and bring to a simmer. Cover and cook gently for about 45 minutes until the lamb is tender.

3 Stir in the saffron and liquid, chickpeas, apricots and pumpkin and cook for a further 10 minutes or until tender, adding a little water if it starts to dry out. Season to taste and serve scattered with coriander.

Asian lamb shanks
This recipe, a slightly lighter, fresher version of slow-cooked lamb shanks, is best served in shallow bowls with rice to absorb the spicy coconut sauce. If the shanks are particularly small, serve two per person.

PREPARATION TIME: 20 minutes

COOKING TIME: 2½–3 hours

SERVES: 4

4 large lamb shanks

2 green chillies, deseeded and roughly chopped

1 onion, roughly chopped

4 garlic cloves, chopped

finely grated rind and juice of ½ lime

1 stalk lemon grass, chopped

15 g (½ oz) fresh root ginger, chopped

2 teaspoons caster sugar

½ teaspoon ground turmeric

15 g (½ oz) coriander, roughly chopped

150 ml (¼ pint) lamb stock

400 ml (14 fl oz) can coconut milk

salt and pepper

chopped coriander, to garnish

shredded spring onions, to garnish

1 Put the lamb shanks in a roasting tin and cook in a preheated oven, 220°C (425°F), Gas Mark 7, for 1 hour until well browned. Drain to a casserole dish. Reduce the heat to 160°C (325°F), Gas Mark 3.

2 Blend the chillies, onion, garlic, lime rind, lemon grass, ginger, sugar, turmeric and coriander in a food processor or blender to a paste, scraping down the mixture from the sides of the bowl if necessary. Blend in the lime juice and stock and pour the mixture over the lamb. Add the coconut milk and cover with a lid.

3 Bake in the oven for 1½–2 hours or until the lamb is tender. Turn the shanks once during cooking. Check the seasoning and serve in shallow bowls, scattered with coriander and spring onions.

Shepherd's pie
This family dish is also a good way of using up leftover lamb from a roast. Roughly chop the cooked meat and add it to the vegetables after frying them with half the stock until just heated through before adding the potato topping.

PREPARATION TIME: 20 minutes

COOKING TIME: about 1 hour 20 minutes

SERVES: 4

2 tablespoons oil

500 g (1 lb) lean minced lamb

1 onion, finely chopped

2 carrots, finely chopped

2 celery sticks, finely chopped

1 garlic clove, finely chopped

1 tablespoon plain flour

300 ml (½ pint) chicken or lamb stock

2 tablespoons tomato paste

400 g (13 oz) can baked beans

1 kg (2 lb) floury potatoes

50 g (2 oz) butter

milk, for mashed potatoes

salt and pepper

1 Heat the oil in a large, heavy-based saucepan and fry the lamb, stirring, until lightly browned. Add the vegetables and garlic and fry for 5 minutes.

2 Stir in the flour, stock, tomato paste and seasoning and heat until bubbling. Cook gently for 30 minutes until the lamb is tender, adding a splash more water if the mixture starts to dry out. Stir in the beans and turn into a shallow ovenproof dish.

3 Meanwhile, cook the potatoes in plenty of boiling, salted water until tender. Drain and return to the pan. Mash well with the butter, milk and seasoning. Spoon the mash over the meat mixture, spreading it in an even layer with a fork. Cook in a preheated oven, 190°C (375°F), Gas Mark 5, for 30–40 minutes until pale golden.

Tip

For a crispy crust pop the pie under the grill before serving, with or without a sprinkling of grated cheese.

Moussaka

Brushing the aubergines with oil and grilling rather than frying them gives a lighter, less 'fatty-tasting' dish. The tangy feta topping is also lovely and light, but you can use a more substantial cheese, like Gruyère or Cheddar, if you prefer.

PREPARATION TIME: 25 minutes

COOKING TIME: 1½ hours

SERVES: 4

500 g (1 lb) aubergines

8 tablespoons oil

1 large onion, finely chopped

500 g (1 lb) lean minced lamb

400 g (13 oz) can chopped tomatoes

1 teaspoon dried oregano

4 garlic cloves, crushed

150 ml (¼ pint) red wine

300 g (10 oz) Greek-style yogurt

2 eggs, beaten

100 g (3½ oz) feta cheese, crumbled

salt and pepper

1 Cut the aubergines into thin slices and arrange them in a single layer on a foil-lined grill rack. Blend 5 tablespoons of the oil with plenty of salt and pepper and brush a little over the aubergines. Grill until golden, then turn and grill again, brushing with more oil. (If necessary, grill in 2 batches.)

2 Heat the remaining oil in a large, heavy-based saucepan and fry the onion and lamb for 10 minutes until browned. Stir in the tomatoes, oregano, garlic, wine and a little seasoning. Cover and cook gently for 20 minutes or until pulpy.

3 Spread a quarter of the meat sauce in the base of a shallow, 2 litre (3½ pint) ovenproof dish and cover with one-third of the aubergine slices. Repeat layering, finishing with the meat sauce.

4 Beat together the yogurt and eggs and spoon over the meat. Crumble over the feta and bake in a preheated oven, 180°C (350°F), Gas Mark 4, for about 45 minutes until the topping is golden.

Pork *Take care to search out a good piece of pork and the results, both in the flavour and the rich juices, will be outstanding. When buying, choose pork that is pale fleshed and glistening with firm, white fat. There's a lot of intramuscular fat in pork, making it quite a rich meat, so a large joint should stretch to a cold platter or sandwiches the next day. Almost any piece of pork can be successfully roasted, but leg and loin are the best and produce delicious crackling.*

Unlike other meats, which can be eaten rare, pork must be cooked through properly before eating, so weigh and calculate cooking times before roasting or use a meat thermometer (see page 8). The juices should run clear when pierced with a knife.

Pork, prosciutto and pepper terrine *A colourful mixture of meat, peppers and herbs packed in a delicious jellied stock is great for a starter or picnic dish. Serve with herb salad and warm bread.*

PREPARATION TIME: 30 minutes

COOKING TIME: 1½ hours

SERVES: 6–8

1 tablespoon vegetable oil

1 kg (2 lb) piece shoulder of pork, skinned

1 glass of white wine

3 red peppers, deseeded and quartered

75 g (3 oz) smoked back bacon, roughly chopped

25 g (1 oz) flat leaf parsley

15 g (½ oz) coriander

75 g (3 oz) pine nuts, toasted

2 teaspoons Tabasco sauce

300 ml (½ pint) jellied veal stock (see page 22)

salt and pepper

1 Heat the oil in a small roasting tin and sear the pork on all sides. Pour over the wine and cover the tin with foil. Bake in a preheated oven, 180°C (350°F), Gas Mark 4, for 1 hour. Add the peppers and bacon to the tin and return to the oven, uncovered, for a further 30 minutes until the meat is cooked through. Drain the meat and peppers, reserving the pan juices in a small bowl, and leave to cool.

2 Cut the meat into pieces, discarding any excess fat. Use a food processor to finely chop the meat in batches. Tip into a bowl.

3 Chop the peppers and bacon into small pieces and finely chop the parsley and coriander. Add to the pork with the pine nuts, Tabasco and seasoning and mix well. Pack into a 1 kg (2 lb) pâté dish.

4 Skim the fat off the meat roasting juices and tip the juices into a small pan with the veal stock. Reheat gently until liquid. Leave until cold but not jellied then pour the stock over the pork. Cover and chill for several hours or overnight.

Pork, prosciutto and pepper terrine

Chunky pork pâté

This is a good, basic pâté recipe in which you can be flexible, substituting chicken, duck or game for the lean pork. Vary the chunkiness by blending the meats lightly or more thoroughly.

PREPARATION TIME: 30 minutes, plus setting

COOKING TIME: 1½ hours

SERVES: 8–10

375 g (12 oz) boneless belly pork, skinned

375 g (12 oz) lean diced pork

250 g (8 oz) chicken livers

125 g (4 oz) smoked streaky bacon, finely chopped

4 tablespoons brandy

1 garlic clove, crushed

1 teaspoon salt

2 tablespoons pink or green peppercorns, lightly crushed

several bay leaves

450 ml (¾ pint) jellied pork or veal stock (see page 22)

1 Roughly chop the belly pork and blend it in a food processor until roughly minced. Tip it into a bowl. Blend the lean pork, then the chicken livers, adding them to the bowl with the bacon, brandy, garlic, salt and peppercorns.

2 Mix the ingredients together thoroughly and pack them into a deep 1 litre (1¾ pint) ovenproof dish. Level the surface and arrange the bay leaves on top.

3 Stand the dish in a roasting tin and pour boiling water into the tin to a depth of 2 cm (¾ inch). Cover with foil and bake in a preheated oven, 160°C (325°F), Gas Mark 3, for 1 hour. Remove the foil and bake for a further 30 minutes or until the juices run clear when pierced with a skewer. Drain off the meat juices (keeping them for another recipe) and leave the pâté to cool completely.

4 Heat the jellied stock in a pan until just liquid and pour it over the pâté until it is completely covered. Cover loosely and chill for up to 3–4 days before eating.

Bacon and celeriac dauphinois

A delicious layering of bacon, potatoes and celeriac is baked in a creamy sauce. Serve with a contrastingly fresh, peppery salad, such as watercress and tomato.

PREPARATION TIME: 20 minutes

COOKING TIME: about 1 hour

SERVES: 4

875 g (1¾ lb) celeriac

750 g (1½ lb) potatoes

250 g (8 oz) dry-cured smoked back bacon

1 tablespoon vegetable oil

1 onion, thinly sliced

300 ml (½ pint) double cream

150 ml (¼ pint) milk

25 g (1 oz) butter

75 g (3 oz) Gruyère cheese, finely grated

freshly grated nutmeg

salt and pepper

1 Cut away the skin from the celeriac and cut the flesh into large pieces, about the size of the potatoes, then thinly slice both vegetables. Bring a large pan of lightly salted water to the boil and tip in the celeriac and potatoes. Return to the boil and cook for 5 minutes until just beginning to soften. Drain and leave to cool slightly.

2 Roughly chop the bacon and fry it in the oil for 4–5 minutes until pale golden.

3 Spread half the celeriac and potatoes in a shallow, 2 litre (3½ pint) ovenproof dish. Scatter with the bacon and sliced onion and arrange the remaining celeriac and potatoes on top.

4 Mix together the cream and milk with a little salt and pepper and pour it over the surface. Dot with the butter and scatter over the cheese. Grate over plenty of nutmeg and cook in a preheated oven, 180°C (350°F), Gas Mark 4, for 45–50 minutes until golden.

Glazed ham

A large joint of gammon does well for family eating (hot one day, cold the next, or in sandwiches) or for a festive dinner. If serving hot, cook potatoes and carrots in the poaching liquid.

PREPARATION TIME: 15 minutes, plus soaking

COOKING TIME: 2 hours 20 minutes–3 hours

SERVES: 8–12

2.5 kg (5 lb) piece gammon

2 onions, sliced

2 carrots, roughly chopped

2 celery sticks, roughly chopped

several sprigs of thyme

4 bay leaves

1 tablespoon peppercorns

8 whole star anise

2 tablespoons orange marmalade

75 g (3 oz) light muscovado sugar

6 kumquats, thinly sliced

1 Soak the gammon overnight in cold water. Drain and weigh to calculate cooking time, allowing 20 minutes per 500 g (1 lb).

2 Put the gammon in a saucepan in which it fits snugly and add the onions, carrots, celery, thyme, bay leaves, peppercorns and 3 of the star anise. Cover with cold water, bring to a simmer, then cover and cook gently for the calculated time. Cool in the liquid for 30 minutes.

3 Drain the meat to a board. Carefully cut away the rind, leaving a layer of fat. Cut diagonal lines across the fat, about 3 cm (1¼ inches) apart, them score lines in the opposite direction.

4 Melt the marmalade in a small pan and stir in the sugar. Spread the mixture over the scored meat. Arrange the kumquats and remaining star anise over the surface and put it in a foil-lined tin. Cook in a preheated oven, 200°C (400°F), Gas Mark 6, for about 20 minutes or until the sugar starts to caramelize. Leave to stand for 20 minutes before serving.

Glazed ham

Bacon steaks with pears and mustard sauce

Use ripe, juicy pears for a lovely contrast with the meat. If you bought the meat from a butcher and it was cut from a large joint soak it overnight before cooking to reduce the saltiness. Serve with a buttery celeriac mash.

PREPARATION TIME: 10 minutes

COOKING TIME: 20–25 minutes

SERVES: 4

2 ripe, juicy pears

4 bacon or gammon steaks

25 g (1 oz) butter, melted

150 g (5 oz) crème fraîche

2 tablespoons finely chopped curly parsley

2 teaspoons grainy mustard

pepper

1 Quarter the pears and arrange them in a roasting tin with the bacon steaks. Brush with the melted butter and season with black pepper. Bake in a preheated oven, 190°C (375°F), Gas Mark 5, for 20–25 minutes or until the bacon is cooked and the pears are soft and juicy.

2 Drain the meat and pears and transfer them to warm serving plates. Add the crème fraîche, parsley and mustard to the roasting tin.

3 Bring the sauce to the boil and let the mixture bubble for a couple of minutes until thickened. Pour it over the steaks and serve.

Pork patties with soured cream and dill sauce

These little patties make a quick and easy supper dish and, once shaped, can be frozen if you don't want to cook them all. Serve with chunky chips and a herb salad.

PREPARATION TIME: 20 minutes

COOKING TIME: 12 minutes

SERVES: 4

500 g (1 lb) lean minced pork

40 g (1½ oz) breadcrumbs

1 small onion, grated

1 teaspoon paprika

1 egg, beaten

8 slices of pancetta or thin rashers of smoked streaky bacon

25 g (1 oz) butter

1 tablespoon vegetable oil

150 ml (¼ pint) soured cream

2 tablespoons chopped dill

2 teaspoons pink or green peppercorns, lightly crushed

salt and pepper

1 Put the pork, breadcrumbs, onion, paprika, egg and a little seasoning in a bowl and mix until evenly combined. This is most easily done with your hands.

2 Divide the mixture into 8 equal pieces and pat them into burger shapes. Wrap a slice of pancetta or streaky bacon around each one, securing it with a wooden cocktail stick.

3 Melt the butter with the oil in a large, heavy-based frying pan and gently fry the patties for 5 minutes on each side until golden. Drain and transfer to serving plates. Add the soured cream, dill and peppercorns to the pan and heat gently, stirring, until smooth and creamy. Season to taste and serve with the patties.

Mustard sausages with sweet potato mash *Use good-quality, lean pork sausages for this recipe. Those with added herbs and garlic are ideal, balancing the sweetness of the glaze.*

PREPARATION TIME: 20 minutes

COOKING TIME: 45 minutes

SERVES: 4

4 tablespoons mango chutney

4 teaspoons grainy mustard

finely grated rind and juice of ½ lemon

500 g (1 lb) lean pork sausages

2 red onions, thinly sliced

2 tablespoons vegetable oil

750 g (1½ lb) sweet potatoes

500 g (1 lb) swede

25 g (1 oz) butter

100 ml (3½ fl oz) chicken stock or water

pepper

1 Finely chop any pieces in the chutney and mix together the chutney, mustard and lemon rind and juice in a small bowl. Put the sausages in a roasting tin and brush them with the mixture. Scatter the onions into the tin and drizzle with the oil. Cook in a preheated oven, 180°C (350°F), Gas Mark 4, for about 45 minutes, basting the sausages once or twice with the juices, until golden.

2 Scrub the potatoes and cut them into chunks. Cut away the skin from the swede and cut it into chunks. Cook the vegetables in separate pans until tender. Drain thoroughly, return to one pan and add the butter and a little black pepper. Mash well.

3 Pile the mash, sausages and onions on to serving plates. Pour the stock into the roasting tin and heat until bubbling, scraping up the residue from the tin. Pour over the mash and serve.

Pork and chorizo casserole

This recipe has a distinctive Spanish flavour, and uses the garlicky, spicy flavour of chorizo sausage to intensify the flavours of the pork and lentils.

PREPARATION TIME: 15 minutes

COOKING TIME: 1 hour 20 minutes

SERVES: 4

175 g (6 oz) green lentils

500 g (1 lb) lean belly or shoulder pork, skinned

4 tablespoons olive oil

150 g (5 oz) chorizo sausage, thickly sliced

2 onions, finely chopped

½ teaspoon ground cumin

3 bay leaves

600 ml (1 pint) pork or chicken stock

500 g (1 lb) potatoes, cut into chunks

1 green pepper, deseeded and chopped

2 garlic cloves, sliced

salt and pepper

1 Rinse the lentils, put them in a saucepan and cover with cold water. Boil rapidly for 10 minutes. Drain.

2 Cut the pork into chunks, discarding any excess fat. Heat 2 tablespoons of the oil in a large, heavy-based frying pan and fry the pork and chorizo, in batches, until lightly browned. Drain and transfer to a casserole dish.

3 Add 1 onion and the cumin and bay leaves to the pan and fry gently until softened. Pour in the stock and bring to the boil. Add to the meats with the lentils and season. Cover and bake in a preheated oven, 160°C (325°F), Gas Mark 3, for 30 minutes. Stir in the potatoes and return to the oven for 30 minutes or until the meat is tender.

4 Meanwhile, heat the rest of the oil in the frying pan and fry the remaining onion with the pepper and garlic until soft. Stir them into the stew, check the seasoning and serve.

Spicy maple ribs

Lengthy cooking ensures that the pork falls easily from the bone and the juices bake to a deliciously dark, sticky glaze. Just remember to baste several times during cooking. Serve these with a watercress or other dark leaf salad and baked potatoes or chunky chips.

PREPARATION TIME: 10 minutes, plus marinating

COOKING TIME: 1½–1¾ hours

SERVES: 4

1.25 kg (2½ lb) meaty pork spare ribs
100 ml (3½ fl oz) maple syrup
2 garlic cloves, crushed
3 tablespoons white wine vinegar
3 tablespoons tomato paste
finely grated rind and juice of 1 lemon
1 red chilli, deseeded and finely chopped
½ teaspoon smoked paprika
salt
lemon or lime halves, to serve

1 Arrange the meat in a single layer in a shallow, non-metallic dish. Beat together the maple syrup, garlic, wine vinegar, tomato paste, lemon rind and juice, chilli and paprika.

2 Pour the mixture over the ribs, turning them until they are completely coated. Cover and marinate in the refrigerator for 4–24 hours.

3 Transfer the ribs to a shallow roasting tin and pour over the excess marinade from the dish.

4 Season lightly with salt and bake in a preheated oven, 180°C (350°F), Gas Mark 4, for 1½–1¾ hours, basting occasionally with the juices, until the meat is tender and the juices are thick and sticky.

5 Transfer to serving plates and serve with lemon or lime halves for squeezing over.

Spicy maple ribs

Jamaican spiced pork
Steeped in a sweet, tangy allspice marinade, these chops or steaks can be cooked over the barbecue, under the grill or in a ridged grill pan. Baked sweet potatoes make the perfect accompaniment, but if you find them too sweet, serve ordinary baked potatoes instead.

PREPARATION TIME: 15 minutes, plus marinating

COOKING TIME: 10–15 minutes

SERVES: 4

3 tablespoons lime juice

3 tablespoons tomato ketchup

2 tablespoons dark muscovado sugar

3 tablespoons vegetable oil

1 teaspoon finely chopped thyme

½ teaspoon ground allspice

3 garlic cloves, crushed

1 red chilli, deseeded and finely chopped

4 pork loin chops or leg steaks

salt

1 Mix together the lime juice, ketchup, sugar, oil, thyme, allspice, garlic, chilli and salt in a shallow, non-metallic dish.

2 Turn the pork in the mixture to coat, then cover and leave to marinate for 1–2 hours.

3 Drain the pork and cook over the barbecue or grill for about 5 minutes on each side or until tender, basting frequently with the marinade.

Pork braised in milk

Cooking a joint of pork slowly and gently in milk is a traditional Italian technique that leaves the meat deliciously moist and succulent. The milk separates during cooking, but is easily strained to make a smooth, creamy sauce.

PREPARATION TIME: 10 minutes

COOKING TIME: 2 hours

SERVES: 5–6

1 kg (2 lb) loin of pork, boned and rolled

3 tablespoons olive oil

1 head fennel, thinly sliced

6 garlic cloves, sliced

small handful sage leaves

900 ml (1½ pints) milk

salt and pepper

1 Season the pork with salt and pepper. Heat the oil in a frying pan and fry the pork on all sides until lightly browned.

2 Scatter the fennel, garlic and sage leaves in a heavy-based pan into which the pork fits quite snugly. Add the pork to the pan, nestling it down into the fennel. Pour over the milk, cover with a lid and cook on the lowest setting for 2 hours or until the pork is tender. (Turn the pork once or twice if it's not completely submerged in the milk.)

3 Drain the pork and keep it warm. Bring the cooking liquid to the boil and boil until reduced. Strain through a fine sieve and serve with the pork.

Pan-fried pork with squash

Any pork steaks work well in this dish, so choose those that look the best when you buy. Use any type of squash; butternut works particularly well.

PREPARATION TIME: 15 minutes

COOKING TIME: about 30 minutes

SERVES: 4

2 teaspoons mustard seeds

¼ teaspoon sea salt

500 g (1 lb) squash

4 boneless pork steaks (e.g., leg, chump or shoulder)

25 g (1 oz) butter

1 tablespoon vegetable oil

1 tablespoon chopped sage

150 ml (¼ pint) chicken or pork stock

100 ml (3½ fl oz) crème fraîche

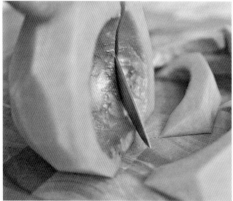

1 Put the mustard seeds in a small, heavy-based frying pan and heat gently until they start to pop or toast. Use a pestle and mortar to crush them lightly with the salt.

2 Cut away the skin from the squash and scoop out any seeds. Cut the squash into chunky slices.

3 Pat the steaks dry on kitchen paper and rub the mustard and salt over the tops.

4 Melt the butter with the oil in a large, heavy-based frying pan and fry the squash on both sides until golden and tender. This will take about 10 minutes. Drain, transfer to a plate and keep warm. Add the pork steaks, spiced side down, and fry for 6–8 minutes until golden. Turn the steaks and add the sage and stock. Cook gently for a further 6–8 minutes until cooked through. Drain and keep warm.

5 Stir the crème fraîche into the pan and cook, stirring, until it is bubbling and slightly thickened. Check the seasoning and serve with the pork and squash.

Pan-fried pork with squash

Pot-roasted pork with lentils

Pork makes a delicious pot-roast, its juices mingling with the garlic, rosemary and wine, which keeps the meat moist and succulent. In winter this is delicious with creamy baked potatoes; in summer serve with buttery new potatoes.

PREPARATION TIME: 20 minutes

COOKING TIME: 2¼ hours

SERVES: 6

225 g (7½ oz) puy lentils, rinsed

1.5 kg (3 lb) joint of pork (e.g., loin or chump end), skinned, boned and rolled

50 g (2 oz) butter

2 tablespoons olive oil

2 onions, sliced

4 garlic cloves, crushed

several sprigs of rosemary

2 tablespoons capers, rinsed and drained

5 anchovy fillets, chopped

200 ml (7 fl oz) white wine

salt and pepper

1 Cook the lentils in boiling water for 20 minutes. Drain and reserve them.

2 Season the meat on all sides. Melt the butter with the oil in a large, heavy-based frying pan and sear the meat on all sides until it is browned. Transfer the pork to a large casserole dish.

3 Add the onions to the pan and fry for 5 minutes. Add the garlic and rosemary sprigs and cook for 1 minute. Tip the onion and herbs into the casserole dish and cover with a lid. Roast in a preheated oven, 180°C (350°F), Gas Mark 4, for 1¼ hours.

4 Tip the lentils around the meat and add the capers, anchovies, wine and seasoning. Return to the oven for a further 30 minutes, then leave to stand for 15 minutes before carving.

Roast pork with apple sauce
Classic roast pork is great for feeding a crowd, and leftovers are delicious served cold with bubble and squeak and pickles. Ask your butcher to score the skin for crackling.

PREPARATION TIME: 30 minutes

COOKING TIME: about 2¼ hours

SERVES: 6

1.75 kg (3½ lb) boned blade or spare rib of pork

1 tablespoon plain flour

300 ml (½ pint) cider

150 ml (¼ pint) pork or vegetable stock

salt and pepper

Stuffing

25 g (1 oz) butter

1 onion, chopped

2 celery sticks, chopped

75 g (3 oz) ready-to-eat prunes, roughly chopped

2 tablespoons chopped sage

50 g (2 oz) breadcrumbs

Apple sauce

50 g (2 oz) butter

3 large cooking apples, peeled, cored and chopped

40 g (1½ oz) caster sugar

6 whole cloves

1 Make the stuffing. Melt the butter in a frying pan and fry the onion and celery for 5 minutes. Stir in the prunes, sage, breadcrumbs and seasoning, then cool.

2 Spread the stuffing over the pork and up, securing at intervals with string (see page 17). Weigh and calculate the cooking time, allowing 30 minutes per 500 g (1 lb). Place in a roasting tin, wipe the skin with kitchen paper and rub plenty of salt into the skin. Roast in a preheated oven, 220°C (425°F), Gas Mark 7, for 30 minutes, then reduce the heat to 180°C (350°F), Gas Mark 4, and cook for the calculated time.

3 Make the apple sauce. Melt the butter and add the apples, sugar, cloves and 1 tablespoon water. Cover and cook over the lowest heat for 20 minutes, until the apples are soft.

4 Drain the pork to a platter and leave to stand. Tip the excess fat from the roasting tin, sprinkle in the flour and cook for 1 minute, scraping up the juices. Add the cider and stock. Bring to the boil, stirring.

Asian roasted belly pork
A lean piece of belly pork will make a delicious yet inexpensive roasting joint. Serve it on a bed of rice with stir-fried vegetables.

PREPARATION TIME: 15 minutes, plus standing

COOKING TIME: 1 hour 10 minutes

SERVES: 5–6

1.5 kg (3 lb) piece belly pork, boned and skinned

1 teaspoon sea salt

½ teaspoon crushed dried chillies

1 teaspoon coriander seeds

2 whole star anise, broken into pieces

½ cinnamon stick, crumbled

8 whole cloves

2 teaspoons caster sugar

2 tablespoons sesame oil

4 small onions, thinly sliced

4 garlic cloves, crushed

4 tablespoons clear honey

3 tablespoons hoisin sauce

1 Use a large, sharp knife to score the pork fat at 1 cm (½ inch) intervals, then score across in the opposite direction.

2 Grind the salt and spices with the sugar in a food processor or coffee grinder. Brush a roasting tin with 1 teaspoon of the oil and put the meat in, scored side up. Rub the spice blend thoroughly into the fat. Cook in a preheated oven, 200°C (400°F), Gas Mark 6, for 30 minutes.

3 Mix the onions with the garlic and remaining oil and spoon them around the pork. Brush the pork with 2 tablespoons honey. Roast for a further 20 minutes. Brush with the remaining honey and cook for a further 20 minutes until the pork is deep golden.

4 Drain the pork and transfer it to a board. Add the hoisin sauce and 100 ml (3½ fl oz) water to the roasting tin and bring to the boil, stirring. Carve the meat and serve with the sauce.

Poultry *Although expensive, a good organic or truly free-range chicken can provide family meals for two or three days, in stark constrast to mass-produced chicken. All poultry should be cooked as soon as possible after purchase and, if stored in the refrigerator for up to two days, unwrapped from its packaging. Remove any giblets and keep them for stock.*

One of the tastiest ways to cook a bird is roasted, with herbs and lemon in the body cavity and a smearing of butter over the outside (except for goose and duck, which are sufficiently covered in natural fat). If using a stuffing, pack it into the neck cavity only (bake the rest in a loaf tin), to allow air to circulate in the body cavity. Chicken, turkey and guinea fowl must be cooked through. If the juices run clear, it is cooked.

Chicken liver and herb pâté

Chicken livers are brilliant for pâté – they are quick to cook and easy to blend to a smooth, creamy consistency. Packed under a buttery seal, the pâté will keep for several days in the refrigerator, perfect for spreading over toast.

PREPARATION TIME: 10 minutes

COOKING TIME: 10 minutes

SERVES: 5–6

500 g (1 lb) chicken livers

125 g (4 oz) butter, softened

1 onion, chopped

2 tablespoons sherry or Marsala

3 pickled onions, drained and finely chopped

1 tablespoon capers, rinsed, drained and finely chopped

2 teaspoons chopped dill

salt and pepper

1 Wash the chicken livers, drain well and pat them dry on kitchen paper.

2 Melt 50 g (2 oz) of the butter in a large, heavy-based frying pan until it is bubbling. Add the onion and fry gently until softened. Add the chicken livers and fry for about 10 minutes, stirring until just cooked through. Stir in the sherry or Marsala.

3 Tip the liver mixture into a food processor or blender and blend until smooth and creamy, scraping the mixture down from the sides of the bowl if necessary. Stir in the chopped pickled onions, capers and dill and season to taste.

4 Pack the pâté into individual serving dishes or into a large pâté dish and press it down in an even layer. Melt the remaining butter and pour it over the surface of the pâté. Cover and chill for at least 2 hours before serving.

Honeyed chicken drumsticks with rösti *This simple, oven-baked supper dish needs only a fresh, leafy salad as an accompaniment. Both the chicken and rösti can be prepared in advance and chilled, ready for popping into a hot oven.*

PREPARATION TIME: 20 minutes

COOKING TIME: 30–35 minutes

SERVES: 4

8 chicken drumsticks

4 tablespoons clear honey

1 garlic clove, crushed

2 tablespoons sun-dried tomato paste

2 tablespoons lemon juice

25 g (1 oz) fresh root ginger, grated

salt and pepper

Rösti

1 small butternut squash, about 500 g (1lb)

300 g (10 oz) potatoes

1 small red onion, finely chopped

3 tablespoons olive oil

1 Put the drumsticks in a small, ovenproof dish into which they fit quite snugly. Mix together the honey, garlic, tomato paste, lemon juice, ginger and a little seasoning and brush the mixture all over the chicken. Leave to stand while you make the rösti.

2 Halve the squash and discard the seeds. Cut away the skin and grate the flesh. Grate the potatoes. Pat the squash and potatoes dry on kitchen paper to remove the excess moisture and mix them in a bowl with the onion, a little seasoning and 1 tablespoon of the oil. Divide the mixture into 4.

3 Shape the rösti into rough cakes with your hands and put them on a small baking sheet. Drizzle with the remaining oil and put them on the lower shelf of a preheated oven, 200°C (400°F), Gas Mark 6, with the chicken on the upper shelf. Bake for 30–35 minutes, turning the chicken in the honey mixture and flipping over the rösti with a fish slice halfway through cooking.

Thai chicken curry

Like many Thai curries, this is quick and easy to make and bursting with lively, aromatic ingredients. Serve in bowls with fragrant Thai rice.

PREPARATION TIME: 25 minutes

COOKING TIME: 40 minutes

SERVES: 4

1 kg (2 lb) boned and skinned chicken thighs
300 ml (½ pint) chicken stock
400 ml (14 fl oz) can coconut milk
3 tablespoons vegetable oil

Curry paste
5 cm (2 inch) piece fresh galangal or root ginger
1 hot red chilli, deseeded and sliced
1 stalk lemon grass
2 garlic cloves, sliced
1 small onion, roughly chopped
small handful fresh coriander
1 teaspoon shrimp paste
½ teaspoon ground turmeric
1 teaspoon cumin seeds
2 teaspoons dark brown sugar
salt

1 Make the curry paste. Peel and roughly chop the galangal or ginger and put it in a blender or food processor with the remaining paste ingredients. Blend to a paste, scraping the mixture down from the sides of the bowl when necessary.

2 Slice the chicken into small pieces and put in a heavy-based saucepan with the stock and coconut milk. Bring slowly to the boil, then reduce the heat to its lowest setting and cook gently for 30 minutes.

3 Heat the oil in a frying pan and fry the curry paste until it is beginning to colour.

4 Stir 2 ladlefuls of the coconut milk mixture into the paste, blending it in until smooth, then pour the mixture over the chicken. Simmer gently for 5 minutes. Check the seasoning and serve.

Thai chicken curry

Chicken parmigiana

Colourful layers of chicken, aubergines and Parmesan in a garlicky tomato sauce make a main meal version of an Italian classic. This is a good dish for assembling in advance, so it's all ready for cooking.

PREPARATION TIME: 25 minutes

COOKING TIME: about 1¼ hours

SERVES: 4

8 tablespoons olive oil

1 onion, finely chopped

3 garlic cloves, crushed

400 g (13 oz) can chopped tomatoes

100 g (3½ oz) tomato paste

2 teaspoons caster sugar

25 g (1 oz) fresh basil, torn into small pieces

500 g (1 lb) aubergines

4 chicken breasts fillets, skinned

125 g (4 oz) Parmesan cheese, grated

salt and pepper

1 Heat 2 tablespoons of the oil in a heavy-based saucepan and fry the onion and garlic for 3 minutes. Add the tomatoes, tomato paste, sugar and seasoning and bring to the boil. Reduce the heat slightly and cook, uncovered, until the sauce is rich and pulpy. Add half the torn basil.

2 Cut the aubergines across into slices 5 mm (¼ inch) thick and place them on a foil-lined grill rack. Brush with a little oil and grill until golden. Turn the slices, brush with more oil and grill again until they are golden.

3 Thinly slice the chicken breasts and fry the meat in the remaining oil until it is cooked through, which will take about 8 minutes.

4 Place one-third of the aubergines in a shallow, 1.8 litre (3 pint) ovenproof dish and cover with one-third of the chicken, sauce, basil and cheese. Repeat the layering, finishing with sauce and cheese.

5 Bake in a preheated oven, 180°C (350°F), Gas Mark 4, for 40 minutes until the cheese is melted and a pale golden colour.

Cassoulet
In a good cassoulet, the beans turn soft and creamy and thicken the meaty juices. For convenience, use fresh duck, or if given more time, the duck confit on page 112.

PREPARATION TIME: 30 minutes, plus soaking

COOKING TIME: about 3½ hours

SERVES: 6

625 g (1¼ lb) dried haricot beans, soaked overnight in water

4 tablespoons olive oil or goose fat

750 g (1½ lb) piece belly pork, skinned and cut into chunks

4 duck legs, halved

8 garlicky sausages

2 onions, chopped

2 bay leaves

1.2 litres (2 pints) chicken stock

4 garlic cloves, crushed

good pinch ground cloves

3 tablespoons tomato paste

75 g (3 oz) breadcrumbs

salt and pepper

1 Drain the beans and put them in a large saucepan. Cover them with cold water, bring to the boil and boil rapidly for 10 minutes. Reduce the heat and simmer gently for 30 minutes until slightly softened. Drain.

2 Heat the oil or fat in a large, heavy-based frying pan. In batches, fry the pork pieces until lightly browned. Drain and fry the duck pieces and sausages until browned.

3 Tip half the beans into a large earthenware pot or casserole dish and scatter over half the meat, half the chopped onions and the bay leaves. Add the remaining beans, meat and onions.

4 Blend the stock with the garlic, cloves and tomato paste and pour the mixture over the beans. Season to taste. Top up with a little water so that the beans are nearly submerged. Cover and cook in a preheated oven, 160°C (325°F), Gas Mark 3, for 2 hours until the beans are completely tender.

5 Scatter the breadcrumbs over the surface and return to the oven, uncovered, for a further 30–40 minutes until golden.

Mascarpone chicken with fennel

This irresistible mixture of mascarpone cheese, garlic and herbs keeps the chicken moist and well flavoured and melts into the cooking juices to make a rich, creamy sauce.

PREPARATION TIME: 20 minutes

COOKING TIME: 40 minutes

SERVES: 4

200 g (7 oz) mascarpone cheese

small handful chervil, chopped

2 spring onions, finely chopped

2 garlic cloves, crushed

4 chicken breasts fillets, skinned

40 g (1½ oz) butter

250 g (8 oz) fennel bulb, thickly sliced

100 ml (3½ fl oz) white wine

40 g (1½ oz) breadcrumbs

salt and pepper

1 Beat the mascarpone with the chervil, spring onions, garlic and seasoning. Make a horizontal slit through the centre of each chicken breast and use half the mascarpone mixture as a stuffing, packing it into the chicken with a teaspoon.

2 Melt half the butter in a large, heavy-based frying pan and fry the fennel until it is lightly browned. Drain and transfer to a shallow ovenproof dish. Fry the chicken breasts on both sides and place them over the fennel. Spread the remaining mascarpone mixture on top.

3 Heat the wine in the pan until it bubbles and pour it around the chicken. Wipe out the pan, melt the remaining butter and use it to coat the breadcrumbs.

4 Sprinkle the breadcrumbs over the chicken breasts and bake in a preheated oven, 180°C (350°F), Gas Mark 4, for about 30 minutes until cooked through.

Poached chicken with tarragon sauce *This recipe is good for chicken thighs, or for breast fillets, as the meat is kept juicy and moist during cooking. Use extra sprigs of tarragon if the ones you've got aren't very leafy.*

PREPARATION TIME: 20 minutes

COOKING TIME: about 45 minutes

SERVES: 4

25 g (1 oz) butter

1 onion, finely chopped

1 celery stick, finely chopped

150 ml (¼ pint) dry white wine

8 large chicken thighs or breast fillets, skinned

600 ml (1 pint) chicken stock

8 large sprigs of tarragon

100 ml (3½ fl oz) double cream

salt and pepper

1 Choose a deep-sided frying pan or sauté pan into which the chicken pieces fit quite snugly. Melt the butter in the pan and fry the onion and celery gently for about 5 minutes until softened.

2 Add the wine and let it bubble for a minute, then add the chicken pieces. Pour over the stock, add half the tarragon sprigs and bring almost to the boil. Reduce the heat to its lowest setting and cover with a lid. Cook very gently for 25–30 minutes until the chicken is cooked through.

3 Drain the chicken and keep warm. Discard the tarragon sprigs and bring the stock to the boil. Boil rapidly until reduced by about half.

4 Pull the tarragon leaves from the remaining sprigs and add them to the pan with the cream. Heat until bubbling, then season to taste and pour over the chicken to serve.

Succulent roast chicken

Packing stuffing under the skin of the chicken is the best way to let the delicious flavours penetrate the meat. It also seeps right through to the juices in the roasting tin so there's plenty of flavour in the gravy. Keep the well-flavoured carcass for stock and the results will be amazing!

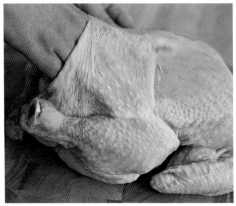

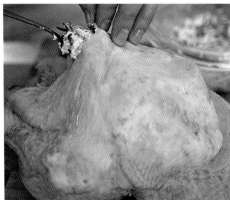

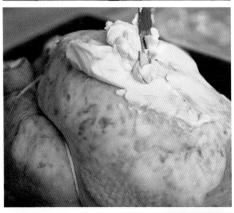

PREPARATION TIME: 20 minutes

COOKING TIME: 1½ hours

SERVES: 5–6

150 g (5 oz) soft goats' cheese

1 hot red chilli, deseeded and chopped

25 g (1 oz) prosciutto, chopped

3 garlic cloves, crushed

2 teaspoons chopped rosemary, plus several extra sprigs

small handful flat leaf parsley, chopped

1.5 kg (3 lb) chicken

50 g (2 oz) butter, softened

1 large glass of white wine

salt

1 Mix the cheese, chilli, prosciutto, garlic, chopped rosemary, parsley and a little salt. Slide your fingers between the chicken breast and skin. Push a little further under the skin to release the skin from the tops of the leg joints.

2 Use a teaspoon to pack the cheese mixture between the skin and the meat. Smooth the skin back into place, at the same time spreading the stuffing in an even layer. Truss the chicken (see page 19).

3 Sit the chicken over the extra rosemary sprigs in a roasting tin and spread with the butter. Roast in a preheated oven, 190°C (375°F), Gas Mark 5, for 1½ hours or until the juices run clear when the thigh is pierced with a skewer.

4 Drain to a serving plate and leave to stand in a warm place for 15 minutes. Add the wine to the roasting tin, stirring to scrape up the residue, and let it bubble for a few minutes. Check the seasoning and serve with the chicken.

Succulent roast chicken

Spatchcocked poussins with herb butter

Flattening or 'spatchcocking' a baby chicken for cooking ensures that all the meat stays moist and succulent, and the melting herb butter more than makes up for its generally mild flavour.

PREPARATION TIME: 10 minutes

COOKING TIME: 25–30 minutes

SERVES: 2

2 spatchcocked poussins

1 tablespoon olive oil

salt and pepper

chive flowers, to garnish (optional)

Herb butter

50 g (2 oz) butter, softened

1 tablespoon chopped chives

1 tablespoon chopped chervil or parsley

1 tablespoon chopped fennel

**finely grated rind of ½ lemon, plus
    1 teaspoon juice**

1 Make the herb butter. Beat together the butter, chives, chervil or parsley, fennel, lemon rind and juice, salt and plenty of pepper.

2 Season the poussins on both sides and brush them with the oil. Cook by grilling, chargrilling or over the barbecue, turning them several times, until they are cooked through, which will take 25–30 minutes. The juices should run clear when the thickest part of the thigh is pierced with a skewer.

3 Transfer to serving plates, top with plenty of herb butter and scatter with chive flowers, if available.

Tip

If you are barbecuing the chicken along with other meats, separate each poussin through the breast bone into halves to make smaller portions.

Thanksgiving turkey

If your turkey has giblets use them to make a well-flavoured stock (see page 23). If not, use a good chicken stock instead. Both this and the sauce can be made several days in advance and chilled or frozen.

PREPARATION TIME: 45 minutes

COOKING TIME: about 3½ hours

SERVES: 8

5 kg (10 lb) turkey, at room temperature

100 g (3½ oz) butter, softened

1 tablespoon plain flour

450–600 ml (¾–1 pint) turkey or chicken stock

salt and pepper

fresh herbs, to garnish

Chilli cranberry sauce

225 g (7½ oz) light muscovado sugar

juice of 1 orange

450 g (14½ oz) fresh cranberries

1 medium red chilli, deseeded and finely chopped

Stuffing

25 g (1 oz) butter

1 onion, chopped

2 celery sticks, chopped

300 g (10 oz) sweet potato, grated

500 g (1 lb) pork sausagemeat

finely grated rind of 1 lemon

15 g (½ oz) chopped herbs (e.g., parsley, oregano, sage, thyme)

1 Make the chilli cranberry sauce. Heat the sugar and orange juice in a saucepan until the sugar dissolves. Add the cranberries and chilli and bring to the boil. Reduce the heat and simmer for 10 minutes until fruit have softened. Cool, then transfer to a dish and chill.

2 Make the stuffing. Melt the butter in a frying pan and fry the onion and celery to soften. Tip into a bowl and cool, then stir in the sweet potato, sausagemeat, lemon rind, herbs and mix well.

3 Rinse the inside of the turkey and pat dry with kitchen paper. Pack the stuffing into the neck cavity and tuck the skin under the bird. Weigh and calculate the cooking time, allowing 20 minutes per 500 g (1 lb). Pack the remaining stuffing into a buttered 500 g (1 lb) loaf tin.

4 Put the turkey in a roasting tin and spread with the butter. Roast in a preheated oven, 220°C (425°F), Gas Mark 7, for 30 minutes. Reduce the heat to 180°C (350°F), Gas Mark 4, and roast for the remaining cooking time, covering with foil as soon as the turkey is golden. Baste frequently during cooking. Put the extra stuffing in the oven for the last hour's cooking. Check that the turkey is cooked. Transfer it to a serving platter, cover with foil and leave to stand for 30 minutes.

5 Tip the excess fat from the tin (reserve it if liked for roasting potatoes and dripping) and sprinkle the juices with the flour. Bubble over a gentle heat, scraping up the pan juices for 1 minute. Add the stock and seasoning and cook, stirring, until lightly thickened. Garnish the turkey with herbs and serve with the stuffing, cranberry sauce and gravy.

Tip

Any accompanying roast potatoes and sweet potatoes can be blanched in boiling, salted water then tossed in oil, or turkey fat (from the tin). Allow about 2 kg (4 lb) total weight and put in the oven about 45 minutes before the turkey is cooked (they can continue roasting while the turkey is left to stand).

Turkey with creole sauce
Frying turkey pieces in a crisp, spicy crumb coat keeps the meat moist and succulent. The pineapple and pepper sauce add a delicious contrast in both texture and flavour.

PREPARATION TIME: 25 minutes

COOKING TIME: 25 minutes

SERVES: 4

500 g (1 lb) piece turkey breast fillet

½ teaspoon paprika

1 tablespoon plain flour

1 egg, beaten

100 g (3½ oz) breadcrumbs

vegetable oil, for frying

salt

Creole sauce

2 tablespoons vegetable oil

1 onion, chopped

2 red peppers, deseeded and chopped

2 garlic cloves, crushed

500 g (1 lb) tomatoes, skinned and chopped

1 small, sweet pineapple, skinned, cored and chopped

2 teaspoons Tabasco sauce

1 Cut the turkey across into 1 cm (½ inch) thick slices then cut each slice into 1 cm (½ inch) strips. Mix the paprika, flour and a little salt and use to coat the turkey.

2 Dip the turkey in the beaten egg and then in the breadcrumbs until coated.

3 Make the sauce. Heat the oil in a sauté pan or large frying pan and gently fry the onion and peppers for 5–8 minutes until softened. Add the garlic, tomatoes, pineapple, Tabasco sauce and a little salt to the pan and cook gently for about 10 minutes, stirring frequently, until pulpy.

4 Heat 1 cm (½ inch) of oil in a pan until a few breadcrumbs gently sizzle. Fry half the turkey pieces in the oil until golden, turning once. Drain while cooking the rest. Serve with the sauce. Add sugar to the sauce if the pineapple isn't very sweet.

Duck confit
Confit, meaning preserve, is the traditional French way of keeping duck without refrigeration for several months. If short of goose fat, you can make up the quantity with a little lard.

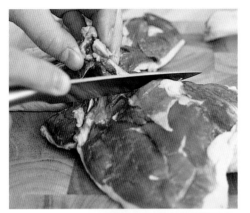

PREPARATION TIME: 30 minutes, plus chilling

COOKING TIME: 2 hours

SERVES: 6

6 large duck legs, about 300 g (12 oz) each
25 g (1 oz) sea salt
1 teaspoon finely chopped thyme
6 garlic cloves, crushed
625 g (1¼ lb) duck or goose fat
2 shallots, finely chopped
300 ml (½ pint) port
100 ml (3½ fl oz) freshly squeezed orange juice
black pepper

1 Cut through the joint of each duck leg. Scrape away the thigh bone and discard. Mix the salt, pepper, thyme and garlic and rub into the skin of each leg. Cover and chill for 24–48 hours.

2 Scrape the salt off the legs and reserve. Melt 1 tablespoon of fat in a heavy-based pan and fry on both sides until golden. Drain into a small casserole dish so they fit snugly. Add the reserved salt mixture and fat. (If solid, melt gently before adding.) Cover and cook in a preheated oven, 150°C (300°F), Gas Mark 2, for 1½ hours. Leave to cool in the fat.

3 Drain the legs to a container. Cover with the fat and chill or store in a very cool place for up to 2 months.

4 Scoop the duck from the fat, scraping off as much as possible, and put in a roasting tin. Cook in a preheated oven, 200°C (400°F), Gas Mark 6, for 20 minutes, until heated through. Drain the fat from the tin and fry the shallots until softened. Add the port and orange juice and cook until reduced by two-thirds. Season and spoon over the duck.

Roast goose with apple and prune stuffing

Although expensive, a goose is one of the easiest birds to roast because the fat keeps it moist and succulent.

PREPARATION TIME: 30 minutes

COOKING TIME: 2½ hours

SERVES: 8–10

25 g (1 oz) butter

1 goose with giblets, about 5.5 kg (11 lb)

2 onions, chopped

pared rind of 1 orange

several sprigs of thyme

2 carrots, roughly chopped

2 teaspoons black peppercorns

200 ml (7 fl oz) port

salt and pepper

Stuffing

500 g (1 lb) floury potatoes, cut into 1 cm (½ inch) dice

25 g (1 oz) butter

1 large onion, chopped

4 tart dessert apples, peeled, cored and chopped

250 g (8 oz) ready-to-eat prunes, roughly chopped

15 g (½ oz) flat leaf parsley, chopped

2 teaspoons chopped thyme

1 Make the stock. Melt 25 g (1 oz) of the butter in a large, heavy-based saucepan and fry the goose neck and gizzards for 5 minutes. Add the onions, orange rind, thyme, carrots, peppercorns and 1.8 litres (3 pints) cold water. Cook very gently for 2 hours.

2 Make the stuffing. Cook the potatoes in boiling, salted water for 10 minutes or until just tender. Drain. Melt the butter in a large, heavy-based frying pan and fry the onion until golden. Add the apples and fry, stirring, for about 8 minutes until golden. Mix with the potatoes and remaining stuffing ingredients. Leave to cool.

3 Pull the lumps of fat from the cavity of the goose and reserve. Thoroughly prick all over the goose skin with a skewer (this will help the fat melt out). Pack the stuffing into the cavity and truss the legs with string. Put the goose on a roasting rack over a large roasting tin and rub the skin with plenty of salt. Place the lumps of goose fat around the goose.

4 Roast in a preheated oven, 220°C (425°F), Gas Mark 7, for 30 minutes. Reduce the heat to 180°C (350°F), Gas Mark 4, and roast for a further 1¾–2 hours or until the juices run clear when a skewer is inserted into the thickest part of the thigh. Transfer the goose to a large platter, cover with foil and leave to stand for 20 minutes.

5 Carefully pour all the fat from the roasting tin into a bowl. Strain the stock into the pan, add the port and bring to the boil. Cook until slightly reduced and glossy. Pour into a jug and serve with the goose.

Tip

This recipe works equally well with a smaller or larger goose. Weigh the bird before cooking, allowing 10 minutes per 500 g (1 lb) at the lower temperature. After cooking at the high temperature, carefully remove the goose from the oven and drain off the fat that will have gathered in the tin. Save it for recipes such as cassoulets or confits. It's also delicious for roasting potatoes.

Braised minted duck

Aromatic herbs and baby vegetables give this casserole a lovely, fresh-tasting, springtime flavour. Serve with plenty of buttery new potatoes.

PREPARATION TIME: 20 minutes

COOKING TIME: 1 hour 40 minutes

SERVES: 6

6 large duck legs, about 300 g (12 oz) each, halved

1 tablespoon plain flour

2 tablespoons olive oil

2 onions, sliced

2 garlic cloves, sliced

1 glass of white wine

600 ml (1 pint) duck or chicken stock

3 bay leaves

4 tablespoons chopped mint

175 g (6 oz) baby broad beans

200 g (7 oz) baby carrots

100 ml (3½ fl oz) double cream

salt and pepper

1 Score the skin of each duck portion several times with a sharp knife. Season the flour and use it to coat the duck legs. Heat the oil in a large, heavy-based frying pan and fry the duck, in batches, until deep golden. Transfer to a roasting tin.

2 Drain off all but 1 tablespoon of the fat and fry the onions and garlic for 3 minutes. Blend in the wine, stock, bay leaves and a little seasoning and bring to the boil. Pour over the duck, cover and cook in a preheated oven, 160°C (325°F), Gas Mark 3, for 45 minutes.

3 Stir in the mint, broad beans and carrots. Re-cover and return to the oven for a further 30–40 minutes until tender.

4 Drain and transfer the duck to warm serving plates. Stir the cream into the roasting tin around the duck and let it bubble on the hob for 2 minutes before serving.

Crispy aromatic duck

This is a simplified version of the traditional technique for cooking an aromatic, tender Chinese duck. It's gently oven-steamed to make it moist and succulent before a final roasting. Like the traditional recipe, serve it rolled in Chinese pancakes with the trimmings.

PREPARATION TIME: 30 minutes, plus overnight marinating

COOKING TIME: 3½ hours

SERVES: 4

2.1 kg (4½ lb) Peking duck (see page 18)
1 tablespoon Sichuan peppercorns
2 tablespoons five-spice powder
2 tablespoons sea salt
4 tablespoons vegetable oil
8 Chinese pancakes
hoisin sauce
½ cucumber, cut into fine matchsticks
1 bunch spring onions, finely shredded

1 Rinse the duck and pat dry with kitchen paper. Grind the peppercorns and mix with the five-spice and salt. Rub the mixture over the duck, wrap in clingfilm and leave it in the refrigerator overnight.

2 Fit a rack over a roasting tin and put the duck on top. Pour hot water to a depth of 5 cm (2 inches) into the tin and cover the duck with a tent of foil. Carefully transfer to a preheated oven, 150°C (300°F), Gas Mark 2, and cook for 2½ hours. Increase the heat to 180°C (350°F), Gas Mark 4.

3 Pour the liquid from the tin and reposition the duck. Brush with the oil and return to the oven, uncovered, for 1 hour or until the skin is crisp. Leave to stand for 20 minutes then cut off the meat, shredding it into small pieces.

4 Reheat the pancakes according to the directions on the packet and serve with the duck, hoisin sauce and vegetables.

Guinea fowl mole

The smallest addition of plain, dark chocolate to a spicy sauce adds a deliciously subtle warmth without dominating the other ingredients.

PREPARATION TIME: 20 minutes

COOKING TIME: 1 hour

SERVES: 3–4

¼ teaspoon ground cloves

1 teaspoon ground cumin

½ teaspoon ground cinnamon

1 guinea fowl, about 1.25 kg (2½ lb), jointed (see page 19)

3 tablespoons vegetable oil

450 ml (¾ pint) chicken stock

40 g (1½ oz) blanched almonds

2 tablespoons sesame seeds

25 g (1 oz) wheat or corn tortilla, torn into pieces

1 large onion, chopped

1 hot red chilli, deseeded and roughly chopped

4 garlic cloves, chopped

15 g (½ oz) plain chocolate (70% cocoa solids)

small handful coriander, roughly chopped

salt

1 Mix the cloves, cumin and cinnamon with a little salt and use the mixture to dust the guinea fowl. Heat 2 tablespoons of the oil in a heavy-based frying pan and fry the pieces on all sides until lightly browned. Transfer the meat to an ovenproof casserole dish. Bring the stock to the boil in the frying pan and pour it over the meat. Cover and cook in a preheated oven, 200°C (400°F), Gas Mark 6, for 45 minutes.

2 Meanwhile, put the almonds, sesame seeds and tortilla in a food processor and blend until finely ground. Heat the remaining oil in the frying pan and fry the onion, chilli and garlic for 3 minutes.

3 Drain the meat from the cooking liquid and keep warm. Ladle a little stock over the dry ingredients in the food processor and blend until smooth. Add this to the onion mixture with the remaining stock.

4 Break the chocolate into the pan with half the coriander and cook gently for 5 minutes, stirring until smooth. Check the seasoning and pour the sauce over the guinea fowl. Serve sprinkled with the remaining coriander.

Pot-roasted guinea fowl with chestnuts *This recipe is given the 'stuffing under the skin' treatment that works so well for milder flavoured poultry dishes, providing plenty of penetrating flavour. Wild mushrooms or chopped walnuts make good alternatives to the chestnuts in the creamy sauce.*

PREPARATION TIME: 15 minutes

COOKING TIME: 1¼ hours

SERVES: 4

1 tablespoon chopped oregano

2 tablespoons chopped flat leaf parsley

finely grated rind of 1 lemon, plus
   1 tablespoon juice

2 garlic cloves, crushed

1 guinea fowl, about 1.25 kg (2½ lb)

25 g (1 oz) butter

1 leek, chopped

300 ml (½ pint) chicken or game stock

12 cooked, peeled chestnuts

4 tablespoons crème fraîche

salt and pepper

1 Mix the herbs with the lemon rind, garlic and seasoning. Slide your fingers between the guinea fowl breast and skin to separate the skin but not pull it away completely. Rub the herb mixture into the meat under the skin and smooth the skin back into place.

2 Melt the butter in a large, heavy-based frying pan and fry the guinea fowl on all sides to brown. Drain and transfer to a casserole dish. Fry the leek in the pan, drain and transfer to the dish.

3 Pour the stock into the pan with the lemon juice and a little seasoning and bring to the boil. Pour the stock over the guinea fowl and cover with a lid. Cook in a preheated oven, 180°C (350°F), Gas Mark 4, for 45 minutes.

4 Stir the chestnuts, crème fraîche and a little seasoning into the cooking juices and cook, uncovered, for a further 20 minutes or until the guinea fowl is cooked through.

Game *Winter is the most abundant time for game, when warming pies, casseroles and dishes with robust gravies are most popular, particularly around the festive season. Ingredients like juniper, chestnuts, mushrooms, celery, bacon, red cabbage and lentils make great companions. Tangy fruit sauces are often served as an accompaniment to venison to counteract the rich flavour.*

When cooking game birds the general rule is that young birds, up to the age of about one, can be roasted (or breasts can be pan-fried) while older birds need more gentle cooking (braising or pot-roasting) to keep them succulent. It's always difficult to assess the age of a bird, so a good supplier is essential. Flavour and tenderness are dependent on how long the game is hung for, and just how 'gamey' that flavour should be is a matter of personal choice.

Quail with lime, chilli and ginger

This quick and easy supper dish is great for preparing several hours (or up to a day) in advance so it's ready for a quick roasting.

PREPARATION TIME: 15 minutes, plus marinating

COOKING TIME: 20 minutes

SERVES: 2

4 quails

1 red chilli, deseeded and finely chopped

2 garlic cloves, crushed

15 g (½ oz) fresh root ginger, grated

2 tablespoons clear honey

1 tablespoon light muscovado sugar

juice of 1 lime

2 tablespoons vegetable oil, plus extra for frying

500 g (1 lb) slender sweet potatoes, scrubbed

salt and pepper

1 Use kitchen scissors or shears to cut off the wing tips from the quails, then cut through each bird, either side of the backbone. Discard the backbone and flatten each quail. Place them in a shallow ovenproof dish into which they fit quite snugly.

2 Mix the chilli with the garlic, ginger, honey, sugar, lime juice, seasoning and the 2 tablespoons of oil. Pour the mixture over the quail, cover with clingfilm and chill until ready to cook.

3 Uncover the quail and roast in a preheated oven, 200°C (400°F), Gas Mark 6, for 20 minutes until the quail is just beginning to brown.

4 Meanwhile, slice the sweet potatoes as thinly as possible. Heat 2 cm (¾ inch) of oil in a large, sturdy frying pan until a slice of potato sizzles on the surface. Fry the potatoes in 2 batches until golden. Drain on kitchen paper.

5 Transfer the quail and chips to warm serving plates and spoon over the juices.

Quail with lime, chilli and ginger

Pigeon breast with port and figs
Topped with a rich and garlicky cream cheese, two pigeon breasts per person should be plenty, particularly if you serve them with a selection of green vegetables.

PREPARATION TIME: 10 minutes

COOKING TIME: about 25 minutes

SERVES: 2

4 pigeon breasts, skinned

25 g (1 oz) butter

1 teaspoon chopped thyme

50 g (2 oz) cream cheese

1 garlic clove, crushed

100 ml (3½ fl oz) port

salt and pepper

4 figs

1 Score each pigeon breast several times with a knife. Melt the butter with the thyme, a little salt and plenty of pepper in a heavy-based frying pan and sear the pigeon on both sides until browned. Transfer the meat to a small, shallow ovenproof dish into which the pieces fit quite snugly. Drizzle with any pan juices.

2 Beat the cream cheese with the garlic. Cut each fig into slices. Spoon the garlic cheese over the pigeon breasts and top with the sliced figs.

3 Pour over the port and cook in a preheated oven, 220°C (425°F), Gas Mark 7, for about 20 minutes until the figs are beginning to colour. Transfer the pigeon to serving plates and keep warm while you make the sauce.

4 Pour the cooking juices into a small saucepan and boil until reduced to a syrupy glaze. Pour the sauce over the pigeon and serve.

Pan-fried pigeon with grapes and walnuts

Pigeon breasts shrink as they cook, so you'll probably need to allow three per person for a main meal. The grapes add a sweetness that's lovely with the sauce. Don't worry about peeling them if you're short of time.

PREPARATION TIME: 15 minutes

COOKING TIME: 15 minutes

SERVES: 2

6 pigeon breasts

25 g (1 oz) butter

2 tablespoons walnut or vegetable oil

25 g (1 oz) broken walnuts

about 300 g (10 oz) red cabbage, finely shredded

1 large shallot, thinly sliced

100 g (3½ oz) green grapes, peeled and halved

200 ml (7 fl oz) chicken or game stock

3 tablespoons double cream

salt and pepper

1 Season the pigeon breasts with salt and pepper. Melt the butter with the oil in a heavy-based frying pan and fry the pigeon breasts for about 2 minutes on each side until they are browned but still slightly pink in the centre. Drain and keep warm.

2 Fry the walnuts in the pan juices until lightly browned. Drain and add the cabbage and shallot to the pan, stir-frying over a gentle heat until softened and just beginning to colour. Return the walnuts to the pan with the grapes and cook, stirring, for 1 minute.

3 Pile the cabbage mixture on to serving plates and top with the pigeon breasts. Add the stock to the pan and bring to the boil, stirring. Cook until reduced by about half. Whisk in the cream and season to taste. Pour the sauce over the pigeon and serve.

Roast pheasant with wild mushrooms

Because it tends to become dry when it's roasted, pheasant is usually wrapped in fat bacon before cooking. This recipe takes the technique one stage further by packing a garlicky pancetta butter under the skin.

PREPARATION TIME: 20 minutes

COOKING TIME: about 1 hour

SERVES: 5–6

75 g (3 oz) butter, softened

75 g (3 oz) pancetta, chopped

10 juniper berries, crushed

3 garlic cloves, crushed

brace of pheasant

2 shallots, finely chopped

300 ml (½ pint) red wine

250 g (8 oz) chanterelles or other wild mushrooms

2 tablespoons redcurrant jelly

salt and pepper

1 Beat 50 g (2 oz) of the butter with the pancetta, juniper berries, garlic and a little seasoning. Slide your fingers between the skin and flesh of 1 of the pheasant breasts to separate the skin but do not pull it away completely. Repeat on the other pheasant. Rub the butter mixture into the meat under the skin, pushing it over the tops of the legs, and smooth the skin back into place.

2 Melt another 15 g (½ oz) of the butter in a large, heavy-based frying pan and fry the pheasants on all sides until golden. Transfer to a large roasting tin.

3 Fry the shallots in the pan until softened and add half the red wine. Bring to the boil and pour around the pheasants. Cover with foil and cook in a preheated oven, 200°C (400°F), Gas Mark 6, for 30 minutes.

4 Meanwhile, fry the mushrooms in the remaining butter. Add to the roasting tin and roast, uncovered, for a further 20 minutes or until the juices run clear when the thickest part of the thigh is pierced with a skewer.

5 Drain the pheasants and mushrooms to a serving platter and add the remaining wine and the redcurrant jelly to the pan. Heat through until the jelly has melted before serving.

Pot-roasted partridge
One whole plump partridge, packed with a stuffing, is the perfect size for a single serving. This recipe also works well for really small poussins, although you might need to extend the cooking time slightly.

PREPARATION TIME: 15 minutes

COOKING TIME: about 1 hour

SERVES: 4

4 small partridges

2 tablespoons hazelnut or vegetable oil

1 small onion, chopped

4 rashers of smoked streaky bacon, chopped

8 ready-to-eat dried apricots, chopped

1 tablespoon chopped sage

25 g (1 oz) blanched hazelnuts, chopped

25 g (1 oz) butter

150 ml (¼ pint) chicken or game stock

150 ml (¼ pint) white wine

100 ml (3½ fl oz) double cream

salt and pepper

sage leaves, to garnish

1 Wipe the partridges and season them inside and out with salt and pepper. Heat 1 tablespoon of the oil in a large, heavy-based frying pan and fry the onion and bacon for 5 minutes until softened. Stir in the apricots, chopped sage, hazelnuts and a little seasoning and mix well.

2 Melt the butter with the remaining oil in the frying pan and fry the partridges until browned. Pack the stuffing mixture into the cavities and put the birds in a small roasting tin.

3 Add the stock and wine to the pan juices and bring to the boil. Pour the mixture over the partridges and cover with a lid or foil. Roast in a preheated oven, 180°C (350°F), Gas Mark 4, for 50 minutes.

4 Transfer the birds to serving plates and keep warm. Add the cream to the pan juices and bring to the boil, stirring. Season to taste and pour the sauce over the partridges. Serve garnished with the sage leaves.

Tea-smoked partridge

Fragrant leaf tea makes a subtly flavoured smoking medium for lighter game meats as well as more everyday meats, such as chicken or guinea fowl. If you don't have a wok with an integral rack use a large, shallow saucepan and fit a small, round rack inside.

PREPARATION TIME: 20 minutes

COOKING TIME: 35 minutes

SERVES: 4

8 partridge breasts, skinned

3 tablespoons strong tea leaves (e.g., jasmine)

3 tablespoons demerara sugar

200 g (7 oz) fragrant rice, plus 4 tablespoons

2 tablespoons sesame oil

2 tablespoons clear honey

2 tablespoons soy sauce

5 tablespoons seasoned rice vinegar

100 g (3½ oz) oyster mushrooms

40 g (1½ oz) fresh root ginger, grated

1 tablespoon sesame seeds, toasted

1 bunch spring onions, finely shredded

3 tablespoons Thai or green basil leaves

1 Score the partridge with a sharp knife. Line the base and halfway up the sides of a wok with foil. Add the tea leaves, sugar and the 4 tablespoons of rice. Heat the wok until the mixture starts to smoke.

2 Fit the rack into the wok and lay the partridge on top. Brush with 1 tablespoon of the oil, cover and smoke for 20 minutes.

3 Mix the remaining oil with the honey, soy sauce and 3 tablespoons of the vinegar in a small ovenproof dish. Stir in the mushrooms. Add the partridge breasts, turning them in the juices, and cook in a preheated oven, 180°C (350°F), Gas Mark 4, for 15 minutes or until tender.

4 Meanwhile, cook the rice. Drain and toss with the ginger, sesame seeds, spring onions, basil and remaining vinegar. Spoon on to serving plates, top with the partridge and mushrooms and spoon over the juices.

Roasted grouse with game chips

Like all game birds, roasted grouse, although delicious, has a tendency to dry out during cooking. Smothering it with butter and a covering of fat bacon helps to counteract this and adds plenty of flavour.

PREPARATION TIME: 15 minutes

COOKING TIME: 25 minutes

SERVES: 4

3 potatoes

4 grouse

75 g (3 oz) butter

small handful thyme sprigs

8 rashers of streaky bacon

vegetable oil, for frying

1 teaspoon plain flour

1 glass of red wine

300 ml (½ pint) game or chicken stock

salt and pepper

watercress, to serve

1 Peel the potatoes and slice them as thinly as possible using a food processor or mandolin. Put the slices in a bowl and cover them with cold water until ready to cook.

2 Put the grouse in a roasting tin and spread butter all over the skin. Push a few thyme sprigs into each cavity and lay the bacon rashers over the birds. Roast in a preheated oven, 220°C (425°F), Gas Mark 7, for 25 minutes, removing the bacon from the birds if it starts to get too crisp.

3 Meanwhile, make the game chips. Drain the potatoes thoroughly and pat them dry on kitchen paper. Heat 3 cm (1¼ inches) of oil in a large, shallow, sturdy pan until a slice of potato sizzles on the surface. Add the potatoes, half at a time, and fry until crisp and golden. Drain to a sheet of kitchen paper and sprinkle with salt and pepper.

4 Transfer the grouse to warm serving plates with the bacon rashers. Stir the flour into the pan juices, stirring with a wooden spoon to scrape up the residue. Add the wine and stock to the pan and cook until the mixture bubbles and is slightly reduced. Serve the grouse with the game chips, watercress and gravy.

Gin-flamed ostrich steaks

If you use a good-quality, tender cut, such as fillet, the steaks can be treated like prime beef and cooked quickly so that the meat is still pink in the centre. Cook a little longer if you prefer, but take care not to overcook or the meat will be too tough.

PREPARATION TIME: 10 minutes

COOKING TIME: 10–12 minutes

SERVES: 4

½ teaspoon crushed black pepper

1 teaspoon chopped thyme

2 teaspoons crushed juniper berries

4 ostrich steaks

1 tablespoon truffle or vegetable oil

3 tablespoons gin

250 g (8 oz) wild or shiitake mushrooms

1 glass of red wine

1 tablespoon redcurrant jelly

salt

1 Mix together the pepper, thyme, juniper berries and a little salt and rub the mixture over both sides of the steaks.

2 Heat the oil in a heavy-based frying pan and fry the steaks for 3–4 minutes on each side until browned but still pink in the centre. Add the gin to the pan and flambé until the flames die down.

3 Drain the meat to warm serving plates and briefly fry the mushrooms in the pan juices.

4 Add the wine, redcurrant jelly and a little salt and let the mixture bubble until the jelly has dissolved. Spoon the sauce over the steaks and serve with sliced, fried potatoes.

Festive game pie

Perfect for making ahead, this pie will sit well in the refrigerator overnight, ready to pop in the oven. Serve any excess stock in a serving jug.

PREPARATION TIME: 45 minutes, plus cooling

COOKING TIME: about 1½ hours

SERVES: 8

450 g (14½ oz) sausagemeat

2 onions, finely chopped

2 teaspoons chopped thyme

75 g (3 oz) butter

400 g (13 oz) lean turkey, diced

4 pigeon breasts, sliced

500 g (1 lb) diced pheasant

2 celery sticks, thinly sliced

3 garlic cloves, crushed

3 tablespoons plain flour

900 ml (1½ pints) game or chicken stock

200 g (7 oz) cooked peeled chestnuts

double quantity shortcrust pastry (see page 25)

beaten egg, to glaze

salt and pepper

1 Mix the sausagemeat with 1 onion and a little thyme. (This is easiest done with your hands.) Shape into 18 small balls.

2 Melt 25 g (1 oz) butter in a frying pan and fry the meatballs until golden. Drain and fry all the meats, in batches, until golden, adding more butter if needed. Drain.

3 Melt the rest of the butter in the pan and fry the remaining onion, celery and garlic. Blend in the flour, add the stock and bring to the boil. Cook for 4–5 minutes.

4 Mix all the meats and chestnuts in a 2 litre (3½ pint) pie dish and pour over enough of the liquid to come to within 2 cm (¾ inch) of the rim. Leave to cool.

5 Cover with the pastry lid and bake in a preheated oven, 190°C (375°F), Gas Mark 5, for 1 hour, covering with foil if the pastry begins to get too brown.

Daube of venison

This hearty, full-flavoured stew adapts well to either braising beef or lamb and to different vegetable additions, such as parsnips, turnips and mushrooms. It's also good with wintry dumplings like those on page 59. Leftovers freeze and reheat well.

PREPARATION TIME: 20 minutes

COOKING TIME: about 1¾ hours

SERVES: 5–6

1 kg (2 lb) lean diced venison

5 tablespoons vegetable oil

2 onions, chopped

3 carrots, diced

2 celery sticks, sliced

100 g (3½ oz) streaky bacon, chopped

4 garlic cloves, crushed

300 ml (½ pint) game or chicken stock

1 glass of red wine

400 g (13 oz) can chopped tomatoes

1 bouquet garni

3 strips of pared orange rind

½ teaspoon ground cloves

salt and pepper

1 Season the meat with salt and pepper. Heat 3 tablespoons of the oil in a large, heavy-based frying pan and fry the meat, in batches, until thoroughly browned, transferring each batch to a large ovenproof casserole dish.

2 Heat the remaining oil in the frying pan and gently fry the onions, carrots, celery and bacon for 5 minutes. Add the garlic and fry for a further 1 minute. Stir in the stock and bring to the boil. Tip the contents of the pan over the meat.

3 Stir in the wine, tomatoes, bouquet garni, orange rind, cloves and a little seasoning and cover with a lid.

4 Cook in a preheated oven, 160°C (325°F), Gas Mark 3, for 1½ hours or until the venison is tender. Check the seasoning before serving.

Venison with blackberry sauce

Tender, succulent fillet or loin steaks are ideal for this dish, although haunch makes a good, if a little firmer, alternative. Serve with some stir-fried green vegetables for the perfect accompaniment.

PREPARATION TIME: 10 minutes

COOKING TIME: 10–12 minutes

SERVES: 2

125 g (4 oz) blackberries (thawed if frozen)
150 ml (¼ pint) game or beef stock
2 venison steaks, about 175 g (6 oz) each
40 g (1½ oz) butter
3 tablespoons cassis
salt and pepper

1 Reserve a quarter of the blackberries and blend the remainder in a food processor with a splash of the stock. Press the purée through a small sieve, preferably non-metallic, into a bowl.

2 Pat the venison steaks dry on kitchen paper and season generously with salt and pepper.

3 Melt half the butter in a frying pan until bubbling, add the steaks and fry for 3–4 minutes on each side until well browned. Drain and transfer to serving plates.

4 Pour the fruit purée into the pan and add the remaining stock. Bring to the boil and cook until the sauce is thick enough to coat the back of a spoon. Add the cassis and reserved butter and berries. Heat through, stirring, until the butter has melted and the sauce is rich and glossy. Serve spooned over the steaks.

Tip

Fry the steaks for 6 minutes on each side if you prefer them well done.

Jamaican curried goat

The cooking time for this creamy, spicy curry will vary depending on the age of the goat. If you can't get goat, lean diced lamb makes a good substitute.

PREPARATION TIME: 20 minutes, plus marinating

COOKING TIME: 1¾–2¾ hours

SERVES: 5–6

1 red chilli, deseeded and finely chopped

50 g (2 oz) fresh root ginger, grated

2 teaspoons ground coriander

2 teaspoons ground cumin

½ teaspoon ground turmeric

750 g (1½ lb) goat, diced

3 tablespoons vegetable oil

2 onions, finely chopped

2 garlic cloves, crushed

2 teaspoons chopped thyme

600 ml (1 pint) chicken or lamb stock

500 g (1 lb) potatoes, cut into cubes

100 ml (3½ fl oz) coconut cream

salt

1 Mix together the chilli, ginger, coriander, cumin and turmeric. Put the goat in a non-metallic dish, add the spice blend and mix together until the meat is coated in the spices. Cover and chill overnight.

2 Heat the oil in a large, heavy-based frying pan and fry the goat, in batches, until golden. Use a slotted spoon to drain and transfer the meat to a casserole dish. Add the onions to the frying pan and fry for 5 minutes.

3 Stir in the garlic, thyme and stock and bring to the boil, scraping up the residue in the pan. Pour the liquid over the meat. Cover and cook in a preheated oven, 150°C (300°F), Gas Mark 2, for 1–2 hours or until the meat is tender.

4 Tip the potatoes into the dish and return to the oven for a further 30 minutes. Stir in the coconut cream and check the seasoning before serving.

Boar and cider casserole

Crushed fennel, plump raisins and tangy cider give the casserole juices plenty of flavour and these are delicious on a bed of creamy mash. Boar has a slightly stronger flavour than pork, but if you can't get hold of any, lean pork would work equally well.

PREPARATION TIME: 20 minutes

COOKING TIME: 1½ hours

SERVES: 4–5

2 tablespoons plain flour

1 kg (2 lb) lean boar, cut into cubes

50 g (2 oz) butter

1 onion, chopped

2 celery sticks, sliced

4 garlic cloves, crushed

1½ teaspoons fennel seeds, crushed

400 ml (14 fl oz) dry cider

200 ml (7 fl oz) chicken or game stock

1 bouquet garni

50 g (2 oz) raisins

salt and pepper

1 Season the flour and use it to coat the boar. Melt half the butter in a large, heavy-based frying pan and fry the meat, in batches, until browned. Use a slotted spoon to drain and transfer the meat to a casserole dish.

2 Melt the remaining butter in the frying pan and fry the onion and celery for 5 minutes until softened. Add the garlic and fennel seeds to the frying pan and fry for 1 minute.

3 Stir in the cider and stock and bring to the boil. Pour over the meat and add the bouquet garni and raisins. Cover and cook in a preheated oven, 160°C (325°F), Gas Mark 3, for about 1¼ hours or until the meat is tender. Season to taste and serve.

Tip

The cooking time will vary depending on the cut of meat, so use the above as a guide.

Rabbit with juniper and pears

A rabbit weighing about 1 kg (2 lb) will be plenty for two people, but will stretch to three if you're serving plenty of accompaniments like buttery mash and green vegetables. Don't discard the liver and kidneys, which can be sautéed in butter, separately, or as part of the dish.

PREPARATION TIME: 15 minutes

COOKING TIME: about 1 hour

SERVES: 2–3

1 tablespoon plain flour

1 rabbit, jointed

50 g (2 oz) butter

1 onion, finely chopped

2 garlic cloves, crushed

1 teaspoon chopped thyme

2 tablespoons Calvados or brandy

10 juniper berries, lightly crushed

150 ml (¼ pint) chicken or game stock

3 small pears

salt and pepper

1 Season the flour and use it to coat the rabbit pieces. Melt half the butter in a sauté pan or large frying pan and fry the rabbit until deep golden. Use a slotted spoon to drain and remove the meat.

2 Add the onion to the pan and fry gently until softened. Return the rabbit to the pan with the garlic and thyme and flambé it with the Calvados or brandy.

3 Stir in the juniper berries and stock and bring to the boil. Reduce the heat, cover the pan and cook on the lowest heat, covered with a lid, for 40–50 minutes until the rabbit is tender.

4 Meanwhile, quarter and core the pears and cut them into chunky slices. Melt the remaining butter in a separate pan and fry the pears until pale golden on both sides. Add them to the rabbit and check the seasoning before serving.

Hare with clementine sauce
Usually very gamey in flavour, hare is a bit of an acquired taste, so this recipe, with its citrus sauce, should have wider appeal than the classic jugged hare.

PREPARATION TIME: 25 minutes, plus marinating

COOKING TIME: about 1¾ hours

SERVES: 4

1 large hare, jointed

3 bay leaves, crumbled

grated rind and juice of 4 clementines

3 garlic cloves, chopped

65 g (2½ oz) butter

150 g (5 oz) bacon lardons

3 tablespoons whisky

leaves of 10 tarragon sprigs

300 ml (½ pint) game or chicken stock

375 g (12 oz) whole baby onions, peeled

1 tablespoon plain flour

salt and pepper

1 Put the hare in a bowl with the bay leaves, clementine rind and juice and garlic. Cover and chill for 3–4 hour.

2 Drain the hare, reserving the juices, and pat dry on kitchen paper. Melt 25 g (1 oz) of the butter in a heavy-based pan and fry the bacon. Use a slotted spoon to drain and transfer the bacon to a casserole dish. Fry the hare, in batches, until browned. Return all the hare to the pan, add the whisky and flambé, then tip into the dish.

3 Add the tarragon to the pan with the stock and strained marinade. Bring to the boil and pour over the hare. Cover and cook in a preheated oven, 150°C (300°F), Gas Mark 2, for 1 hour. Meanwhile, fry the onions in another 15 g (½ oz) butter until beginning to colour, add to the hare and cook for a further 30 minutes.

4 Drain to plates and pour the juices into a pan. Blend the flour with the remaining butter and add to the pan, whisking well. Season and spoon over the hare.

Hare with clementine sauce

Index

Acknowledgements

Photography: © Octopus Publishing Group Ltd / Stephen Conroy

Executive Editor Sarah Ford
Editor Kate Tuckett
Executive Art Editor and Design Karen Sawyer
Senior Production Controller Martin Croshaw
Photographer Stephen Conroy
Food Stylist Joanna Farrow
Props Stylist Rachel Jukes